# The Making of a Modernist

The Making of a Modernist:

# GERTRUDE STEIN

from *Three Lives* to *Tender Buttons*

Jayne L. Walker

The University of Massachusetts Press
Amherst, 1984

Copyright © 1976, 1984 by Jayne L. Walker
All rights reserved
Printed in the United States of America
LC 83–18184   ISBN 0–87023–323–8
Library of Congress Cataloging in Publication Data
appear on the last page of this book.

Publication of this book was assisted by the
Council of Learned Societies under a grant from the
Andrew W. Mellon Foundation.

Acknowledgment is made to the following and to
the Estate of Gertrude Stein for permission to
reprint selections from published material under
copyright:
From *Selected Writings of Gertrude Stein*, ed. Carl
Van Vechten, copyright 1946 by Random House,
Inc., and from *Three Lives*, by Gertrude Stein,
copyright 1909 and renewed 1937 by Gertrude
Stein. Reprinted by permission of Random House,
Inc.
From *Two: Gertrude Stein and Her Brother and
Other Early Portraits*, by Gertrude Stein (Yale
University Press, 1951). Reprinted by permission of
Yale University Press.

To the memory of
Bertel Pedersen
1943–1978

# Acknowledgments

MANY friends and colleagues have advised and supported me in various ways during the course of this project. To Richard Bridgman, Bertrand Augst, Thomas Parkinson, Eric Johannesson, Robert Alter, Françoise Meltzer, David Miller, Francine Masiello, Joyce Cole, and Anne Oja, my sincere appreciation. I am especially indebted to Leon Katz, who generously shared with me his transcripts and chronology of Stein's unpublished "Notebooks" and his vast store of information concerning the early period of her career, and to Donald Gallup, former curator of the Yale Collection of American Literature, and the staff of the Beinecke Library for their assistance in my research.

I also appreciate the cooperation of the Beinecke Rare Book and Manuscript Library's Collection of American Literature and the Estate of Gertrude Stein, in granting me permission to quote from Stein's unpublished manuscripts.

The Committee on Research and the Departments of English and Comparative Literature at the University of California, Berkeley, granted me both the time and the financial support necessary to complete the final version of this study. I have long been grateful for their support of my research.

My only regret is that Bertel Pedersen did not live to see the completion of this book which he influenced in so many ways. *The Making of a Modernist* is dedicated to the memory of this exemplary scholar of literary modernism.

Contents

# KEY TO CITATIONS OF STEIN'S TEXTS

ABT  *The Autobiography of Alice B. Toklas.* 1933; rpt. New York: Random House, 1960.

EA  *Everybody's Autobiography.* 1937; rpt. New York: Random House, 1973.

GP  *Geography and Plays.* Boston: The Four Seas Company, 1922.

GMP  *G.M.P.,* in *Matisse, Picasso and Gertrude Stein with Two Shorter Stories.* 1933; rpt. Barton, Berlin, Millerton: Something Else Press, 1972.

JHHPP  *Jenny, Helen, Hannah, Paul and Peter,* in *Two: Gertrude Stein and Her Brother and Other Early Portraits.* New Haven: Yale University Press, 1951.

LGB  *A Long Gay Book,* in *Matisse, Picasso and Gertrude Stein with Two Shorter Stories.*

LIA  *Lectures in America.* 1935; New York: Random House, 1975.

MMW  *Many Many Women,* in *Matisse, Picasso and Gertrude Stein with Two Shorter Stories.*

MOA  *The Making of Americans.* 1925; rpt. New York: Something Else Press, 1966.

NB  Unpublished notebooks in the Yale Collection of American Literature (YCAL).

PP  *Portraits and Prayers.* New York: Random House, 1934.

P  *Picasso.* 1938; rpt. Boston: Beacon Press, 1959.

QED  *Q.E.D.* 1950; rpt. in *Fernhurst, Q.E.D. and Other Early Writings.* New York: Liveright, 1971.

SW  *Selected Writings of Gertrude Stein,* ed. Carl Van Vechten. New York: Random House, 1962.

TB  *Tender Buttons.* 1914; rpt. in *Selected Writings of Gertrude Stein.*

TI  "A Transatlantic Interview 1946," in *A Primer for the Gradual Understanding of Gertrude Stein,* ed. Robert Bartlett Hass. Los Angeles: Black Sparrow Press, 1971.

TL  *Three Lives.* 1909; rpt. New York: Random House, 1936.

T  *Two: Gertrude Stein and Her Brother,* in *Two: Gertrude Stein and Her Brother and Other Early Portraits.*

Introduction

FROM *Three Lives* (1905–6) to *Tender Buttons* (1912), Gertrude Stein created a series of texts that engage, early and radically, what we have come to recognize as the most crucial issue of modernist art—the problem of representation. *Three Lives* was her first major assault on the conventions governing literary representation in the nineteenth century. This text, in which the halting, repetitive uncertainties of colloquial speech supplant the authoritative voice of conventional narrative discourse, gradually came to be regarded as a central force in reshaping the tradition of American fiction in the twentieth century. Long before *Three Lives* received that belated recognition, however, Stein had gone on to invent far more radical ways of manipulating language to create ever-closer approximations of "reality" as she defined and redefined it. By 1912 her uncompromising efforts to embody her sense of reality in language culminated in *Tender Buttons*, the iconoclastic text in which "real is only, only excreate, only excreate a no since" (TB, 496).

*Tender Buttons* is both a manifesto and a demonstration of the new mode of writing that it announces. "Act so that there is no use in a center" (TB, 498)—this imperative produces a text that enacts the principles of fragmentation and difference and celebrates the freeplay of writing as a combinative game limited only by the systemic laws of language. If these principles seem to echo the poststructuralist characterizations of the modernist text that have already become clichés of contemporary literary criticism, it is no less remarkable to find them so explicitly thematized and so rigorously enacted in Stein's 1912 text. By the time she wrote *Tender Buttons*, she had already embraced the major premises that would shape most of her subsequent work: the epistemological model of present-tense vision, unmediated by memory or habitual associations, and the literary strategy of subverting, defying, or simply denying the normal discursive order of language. Although she continued to write prolifically for more than thirty years, inventing countless ways to "excreate a no since," no subsequent period of her work exhibits either the range of formal invention or the intense reexamination of fundamental aesthetic principles that impelled the extreme and rapid stylistic changes in her work from *Three Lives* to *Tender Buttons*.

Precisely how and why did this writer who set a new standard for colloquial realism in *Three Lives* come to flaunt the radical iconoclasm of *Tender Buttons* only a few years later? Surely this is the single most compelling question posed by Stein's career as a modernist writer. In her later theoretical writings, Stein herself always claimed that everything she wrote was equally motivated by an "intellectual passion for exactitude in the description of inner and outer reality" (ABT, 211). But she was equally adamant in her insistence that "reality" is a dynamic configuration that changes from one century—and one generation—to the next: "One must never forget that the reality of the twentieth century is not the reality of the nineteenth century, not at all" (P, 21).

This is the kind of polemical appeal to the "real" that has characterized avant-garde art since the mid-nineteenth century, as successive assaults on artistic conventions have been launched in the name of the uncoded "reality" that lies outside *vraisemblance*. Both challenged and reassured by these claims, the viewing public long ago learned to recognize the images that Cézanne, Picasso, and other painters created as new ways of seeing and rendering the world. In the case of Stein's writings, however, readers who encounter so little in the texts she wrote after *Three Lives* that they can *recognize* as realistic find it extremely difficult to understand what "realities" her increasingly unconventional texts engage and how they do it.[1]

The more radically a literary text departs from familiar conventions, the more actively the reader must struggle to determine how to read it. How does it "work"? What are the theoretical premises that shape its formal strategies? Nowhere is the question of artistic intention, in this sense, such a pressing concern as in the encounter with a new artistic work that systematically refuses to conform to traditional expectations. Faced with the extreme unconventionality of Stein's texts, many readers have simply declared them "meaningless." The more intrepid have generally sought the keys to their significance elsewhere—in Stein's later theoretical writings or, even more frequently, in cubist painting or Jamesian psychology.[2]

Both the retrospective theoretical statements that Stein began to issue in the twenties and the ever-popular legend of her intimate involvement with modernist painting and Jamesian psychology have frequently been mined for evidence of the "influences" that shaped her work during the early years of her career. No study of her literary production fails to acknowledge these affinities or to suggest that, somehow, one or another of these extrinsic models will explain the difficulties of her enigmatic texts. As early as 1912, Alfred Stieglitz, who published Stein's portraits of Picasso and Matisse in his influential magazine *Camera Work*, suggested that her texts proffered a "Rosetta stone of comparison; a decipherable clew to that intellectual and esthetic attitude which underlies and inspires the [modernist] movement."[3] Instead of approaching Stein's texts in this way, as "decipherable clews" that could elucidate the premises of modernism, Stein's critics have generally employed the opposite procedure, turning to modernist painting and Jamesian psychology for clues to the intentions that inform Stein's texts. This procedure, which has dominated the history of reception of Stein's writings, has given rise to strikingly different —and sometimes mutually contradictory—accounts of her intentions, all of which equally short-circuit any serious effort to decipher her texts in their own terms.

Until recently, many of Stein's critics simply ignored her professed commitment to "reality" in favor of the assumption that she was emulating the premises and methods of "abstract," nonobjective painting. This historically untenable assumption, which went virtually unchallenged until a few years ago, long served as the most serious impediment to deciphering Stein's difficult texts.[4] The opposite approach has long been to endorse Stein's claims to "realism" by regarding her most unconventional texts as direct notations—or faithful re-creations—of the Jamesian stream of consciousness. Although Jamesian psychology can help to clarify the epistemological assumptions that Stein's writings explore, it has evident limitations as an interpretative model. Purporting to offer a global explanation of her writings, it tends to discourage interpretation as effectively as the model of nonobjective painting. While the one assumes that the language of the text is totally opaque, the other posits the ideal transparency of pure naturalism. But that assumed transparency is equally uninterpretable, because this model locates the meaning of these surface manifestations in the irrecoverable private associations of the moment—and the mind—that created it. Even when Stein's writings are regarded as more general demonstrations of the operations of consciousness, this psychological approach tends toward the conclusion that they belong to the "phenomenology of mind, not to literature," as Allegra Stewart asserts in her Jungian analysis of Stein's works.[5]

Stein's later theoretical writings, with their relentless emphasis on composition as a present-tense process liberated from the preconceptions of memory, lend some support to this account of her texts as naturalistic renderings of the movements of consciousness. But in her equally strong insistence that "[l]anguage as a real thing is not imitation either of sound or colors or emotions it is an intellectual recreation and there is no possible doubt about it" (LIA, 238), she clearly acknowledges that her commitment to the reality of immediate experience was always matched by—if not mastered by—her intense awareness of the separate but equal reality of language.

The lectures and other theoretical works Stein began to write in the late twenties have been among the most popular and influential of her literary productions. Many critics have used them as shortcuts to understanding her more difficult texts, which allow them to be read as demonstrations of the theories of composition and time that the essays present in a relatively straightforward style. This approach, too, has its pitfalls, especially as a way of dealing with the texts that preceded Stein's wholehearted embrace of present-tense composition in *Tender Buttons*. These later writings, which have more polemical force than theoretical precision, systematically refuse to acknowledge how fundamentally both her conception of reality and her evaluation of the powers and limitations of language changed during the early years of her career. For this reason, they tend more to obscure than to clarify the terms of her exploration of the problem of representation from *Three Lives* to *Tender Buttons*.

In these essays, Stein attempted to provide a unifying theoretical framework for all of her writings by reinterpreting her early texts as a steady progress toward the theory and practice of present-tense composition that dominated her writings beginning in 1912. The first essay, "Composition as Explanation," inaugurates this strategy by claiming that as early as *Three Lives* she had "naturally" created a "prolonged present" that prefigures the "continuous present" of *The Making of Americans* and all her subsequent writings. Denying that the seismic changes in her work between *The Making of Americans* and *Tender Buttons* have any particular significance, Stein declares that both are equally "natural" consequences of this uniform immersion in present-tense experience: "if it is all so alike it must be simply different and everything simply different was the natural way of creating it then" (sw, 519). In "Portraits and Repetition" and "The Gradual Making of *The Making of Americans*," she presents a more detailed account of the premises that guided her efforts to render the essential qualities of personality in these early works; but again she refuses to provide an adequate explanation for the radical reversal of these premises by the time she wrote *Tender Buttons*. The latter essay proffers a series of six quotations from *A Long Gay Book*, one of the transitional texts that spans these two phases of her writing, in order to "show how it changed, changed from Making of Americans to Tender Buttons" (LIA, 153). But even while asserting that this was a "necessary change," she again evades the question of why it was necessary, with a flippant refusal to acknowledge the magnitude of the issues that were at stake. Why after years of struggling to render the underlying mechanisms of human character in terms of a totalizing unity did she come to celebrate the principle of pure difference? And what considerations led her to abandon her efforts to make language embody essential truths of human experience for the systematic subversion of sense in *Tender Buttons* and the texts that followed?

It is the evident failure of her later essays to explain this fundamental reorientation that has encouraged so many critics to conclude that it must have been the result of her imitation of modernist painting. John Malcolm Brinnin was the first to suggest that the dramatic change from the austere, repetitive prose of *The Making of Americans* to the logically disjunctive sentences of *Tender Buttons*, bristling with concrete nouns and adjectives, parallels what art historians have identified as the two phases of cubism—the analytic and the synthetic—that Picasso and Braque created between 1909 and 1912.[6] Wendy Steiner more fully elaborates these parallels in her recent book *Exact Resemblance to Exact Resemblance: The Literary Portraiture of Gertrude Stein*. While Steiner's book corrects the widespread misunderstanding that Stein was modeling her work on nonrepresentational painting and, consequently, makes resolute efforts to decipher Stein's texts, it concludes, too readily, that Stein was attempting a misguided "translation of pictorial norms into literary ones" during these years.[7] Steiner thus endorses the most common explanation of Stein's literary evolution, which regards the modernism of *Tender Buttons* and other texts as at best derivative, dependent upon innovation in another medium, and at worst a failure, predicated upon a naïve or perverse refusal to acknowledge the inherent differences between the resources of painting and those of literature.

Interestingly, one of the few challenges to this negative assessment comes from an art historian. In a little-known 1974 essay David Antin argues that Gertrude Stein was the only thoroughly modernist writer in English, because she was the only one who rigorously practiced what art historians recognize as the central axiom of modernism: "that it is necessary to begin from a radical act of definition or redefinition of the domain of the elements and the operations of the art or of art itself."[8] From this perspective, *Tender Buttons* is not derivative from painting but a logical product of Stein's parallel investigation of the same fundamental issue that preoccupied first Cézanne and then Picasso and Braque: the

problem of representation, redefined in terms of the distinctive resources of their medium.

By charting the course of this modernist project in Stein's writings from its beginnings in *Three Lives* to its culmination in *Tender
Buttons*, my study clarifies the internal logic that underlies the extreme changes in her formal strategies during the early years of her
career. Instead of relying on Stein's later essays as a guide to the
theoretical concerns that shaped her work from 1905 to 1912, my
analysis focuses on the texts she wrote during this period, many of
which have barely begun to be read. The unpublished notebooks
and manuscript notations Stein inscribed during this period provide crucial evidence of the theoretical concerns and working methods that shaped her early work.[9] But it is the texts themselves—
especially *Three Lives, The Making of Americans*, the portraits of
artists, *Two*, and *Tender Buttons*—that most fully articulate the
theoretical concerns that motivate their changing styles. Imprecise
dating of the works Stein produced during this period of extreme
and rapid stylistic change, plus the presence of several styles in
single texts, have caused these various phases to be regarded as
a synchronic array of formal possibilities rather than as successive
stages in an ongoing process of exploration.[10] When they are read
in the order of their production, these formal strategies appear in
rigorous chronological sequence, and each new style is anticipated
by a prior articulation of the theoretical concerns that would soon
impel a major formal innovation.

Stein's unpublished notebooks, which record her extensive
commentaries on the painters whose work interested her most,
amply confirm the crucial role of modernist art as a catalyst for her
own investigations of the problem of representation in language.
But they reveal that scholarly studies of the impact of painting on
her work, which have always focused primarily, if not exclusively,
on Picasso's cubism, have been somewhat misdirected. My reas-
sessment of Stein's relationship to painting is firmly grounded in
contemporaneous formulations of the dominant aesthetic issues in
the Parisian art world during these years. Stein's own notebooks
provide persuasive evidence that it was Cézanne's legendary dedi-

cation to "realizing" his sensations that served as the seminal model not only for *Three Lives* but for all her subsequent work as well. Even during the years of Stein's greatest intimacy with Picasso, she continued to regard Cézanne as the "great master," while what she admired most in Picasso's work was the extent of his adherence to the aesthetic principles of Cézanne.

Because Stein's notebooks so clearly identify Cézanne's crucial role in the formation of her own aesthetics, I begin this study with a chapter that explores the formal and theoretical consequences of Cézanne's efforts to create what Stein saw as a "direct relationship to the object" (NB-A, 14) and the implications of this project for an artist whose medium is language. By demonstrating how closely Cézanne's compositional techniques accord with William James's descriptions of the process of visual perception, this chapter reveals how perfectly Stein's early training in Jamesian psychology prepared her to understand Cézanne's new mode of realism and its potential significance for the problem of representation in writing.

The most compelling evidence of the enormous impact of Cézanne's painting on Stein's work is the transformation of her writing from *Q.E.D.* (1903) to *Three Lives*. Begun a year after her initial confrontation with Cézanne, *Three Lives* is the first of many texts that resulted from Stein's resolve to reinvent literary realism on new foundations, grounded in "direct" experience and embodied in the material patterning of language. During the next few years this project entailed both a continuing revaluation of the semiotic resources of language and a series of redefinitions of those aspects of language that could be "figured" in language.[11]

By 1912 Stein's relentless pursuit of reality in and through language had led her, with its own inexorable logic, to *Tender Buttons*, her brilliantly subversive demonstration of the unbreachable gulf that separates the chaotic plenitude of the sensory world from the arbitrary order of language. In the same year Picasso's exploration of the conditions and limitations of pictorial representation had reached a similar culmination in cubist *collage*, with its provocative explorations of how far the iconography and syntax of painting can depart from the order of natural appearances and still signify elements of external reality. But the powerful internal coherence of Stein's writings from *Three Lives* to *Tender Buttons* suggests that these similarities cannot be explained merely as Stein's imitations or translations of Picasso's most recent work. They must be understood, instead, as parallel derivations from Cézanne, their common point of departure.

Between 1905 and 1912 Stein was engaged in a monumental struggle with the problem of realism, in which she worked through successive revaluations of the issue of representation that parallel the course of modernist painting from Cézanne to cubist *collage*. In painting, E. H. Gombrich has argued, it was the ideal of the "innocent eye"—the demand for ever-greater fidelity to immediate sensory data—that led, inevitably, to the breakdown of the long tradition of illusionistic painting.[12] Cézanne was the crucial pivotal point in this historical process; it was his techniques of activating the surface patterning of the canvas to encode the multiple and contradictory signs of visual perception that laid the groundwork for the cubists' deliberate attenuation of the connection between pictorial signs and perceptual reality. Unlike Picasso, Stein wholeheartedly embraced Cézanne's legendary ideal of "realizing" his sensations in terms of the material resources of the medium. Far from merely following Picasso's lead during these years, she struggled desperately to retain her faith that language could be manipulated to embody the structures and rhythms of reality. By the time she wrote *Tender Buttons*, she had accepted the inevitable defeat of this ideal and gone on to create a new art from the ruins of this Cézannesque dream of capturing reality in the lineaments of language. As the terms of her successes and her failures are better understood, the trajectory of Stein's writings from *Three Lives* to *Tender Buttons* should come to be regarded as a crucial episode in the history of representation.

The "Reality" of Cézanne and Caliban

BELIEVE in reality as Cezanne or Caliban believe in it" (NB-D, 11). This credo, which Stein recorded in her 1909 working notebooks, provocatively couples the modernist painter with Shakespeare's ignoble savage to invoke a "reality" that lies far outside conventional *vraisemblance*. In painting as well as in literature, verisimilitude depends more on correspondence to conventional models than on accurate notation of the immediate data of perception. In *The Autobiography of Alice B. Toklas*, Stein recalled that Cézanne's portrait of his wife had not at first "*seemed* natural, it had taken her some time to feel that it *was* natural" (35; my emphasis). Once she understood that Cézanne's paintings represented a version of the real that had not previously been codified by tradition, she dedicated herself to an equally radical pursuit of "reality" in her own writing.

In Stein's 1909 credo, we can already see the paradoxical tension inherent in this project. At the beginning of *The Tempest*, Caliban's natural world has already been transformed into Prospero's stage. Prospero's language and stagecraft, his civilizing powers, all function as instruments of Caliban's oppression. Within the play, Caliban has no words to speak his reality; his only language is his oppressor's: "You taught me language and my profit on't / Is, I know how to curse!"[1] Reduced to curses and to wordless gestures of rebellion, Caliban's physical force is contained by Prospero's magic, but his stubborn, speechless "reality" remains outside Prospero's powers to civilize and to reconcile. At the end of the play, when the other characters return to the civilized world, Caliban remains on the island. His own speech, in his own world, remains unwritten, unimaginable within the world of Shakespeare's drama. To give speech to Caliban, to a "reality" that lies this far outside *vraisemblance*—this goal must eventually lead to radical subversion of the laws of language that forbid Caliban his own authentic speech.

While Caliban suggests an evocative metaphorical model, Cézanne's canvases provide a more concrete point of departure for studying the formal and theoretical consequences of Stein's radical commitment to "reality." "Primitive," even "savage," were the labels critics most frequently bestowed on Cézanne's art at the time Stein first became interested in his work. His rendering of "people, landscapes, and still-lifes just as he saw them, without troubling himself about imparting a little beauty," shocked most viewers, who judged that in his paintings "[f]aces, trees, flowers, fruit, or furniture were bungled with the same brutality."[2] While critics generally recognized his "scrupulousness in the presence of nature," most deplored the deviations from traditional models that it entailed. His violations of scientific perspective and chiaroscuro modeling, his rough, obtrusive brushstrokes, and his distortions of shapes and outlines of objects led admirers and detractors alike to characterize his work as "primitive."

By the time Stein began to interest herself in Cézanne's work, a new generation of painters was beginning to recognize the revolutionary implications of his compositions. Stein occupied an ideal vantage point for understanding the nature of the challenge that his paintings posed to the tradition. In 1904 she and her brother Leo, an aspiring aesthetician and art historian, had "discovered" Cézanne under the tutelage of Bernard Berenson, the Renaissance art historian, and Charles Loeser, an early collector of his work. That year the Steins bought four of his paintings, including the portrait of Mme Cézanne, which Stein later claimed as her major inspiration for writing *Three Lives*. In the same year Emile Bernard published a collection of Cézanne's "opinions." These and other quotations that began to appear in articles devoted to his work corrected the assumption that he was a genuine naïf, ignorant of conventional techniques, and clarified the theoretical premises that shaped his paintings. In 1905 the Steins' purchase of Matisse's controversial *Woman with the Hat* and, a few weeks later, of Picasso's *Young Girl with Flowers* inaugurated their collection of contemporary painting and their intimate friendship with these two painters as well. The Steins' atelier soon became "charged with the atmosphere of propaganda" (in Leo's words), as an increasing number of visitors came to see the paintings and hear Leo and the painters discuss the aesthetic concerns that were generating the new art Picasso and Matisse were creating.[3]

For a number of years before 1905, Matisse had been studying the paintings of Cézanne and using some of his techniques in his own work. Even during his fauvist period, his brilliant use of color, so different from Cézanne's palette, was accompanied by a Cézannesque construction through color planes. By 1907, however, Matisse had begun to depart from Cézanne's rendering of three-dimensional space to explore a flatter, more decorative patterning of bold colors, while Picasso had embarked on his own reinterpretation of Cézanne in *Les Demoiselles d'Avignon*. In 1905 Matisse was widely recognized as the leader of the French avant-garde painters while Picasso was virtually unknown. When interest in Cézanne's painting intensified after his death in 1906, Picasso was recognized as the heir to his tradition. Although Matisse himself regarded Cézanne as "le père de nous tous," many of the avant-garde painters rejected Matisse's increasingly flat, decorative painting to pursue the new direction suggested by Picasso's reinterpretation of Cézanne.[4] In 1906 Stein herself still regarded Matisse as the leader of the new movement in painting. In a letter written that year, she described *Three Lives*, which she later maintained was inspired solely by Cézanne's work, as a "noble combination of Swift and Matisse."[5] But after 1907, when Picasso and Matisse began to pursue radically divergent goals in their work, Stein became a passionate partisan of Picasso's art.

Stein's working notebooks reveal that in 1909 she regarded Cézanne as the "great master of the realization of the object itself" and Picasso as the only contemporary artist who was successfully following Cézanne's aesthetic program (NB-A, 14). Cézanne's dicta, published by Bernard in 1904, reiterate the painter's extreme dedication to the goal of "realizing" [*réaliser*] his sensations: "To paint after nature is not to copy the objectively given; it is to realize one's sensations."[6] The legend of Cézanne's lifelong struggle to "realize" his sensations was an essential part of his appeal for Stein, as well as for the painters who were her contemporaries. Years later, Picasso commented, "It's not what the artist *does* that counts but what he *is*. Cézanne would never have interested me a bit if he had lived and thought like Jacques Emile Blanche, even if the apple he painted had been ten times as beautiful. What forces our interest is Cézanne's anxiety—that's Cézanne's lesson."[7] Stein's repeated insistence on her own intense struggles to "realize" her characters throughout *The Making of Americans* indicates how thoroughly she identified her own goals with Cézanne's at that time.

While she was working on *The Making of Americans* in 1909, Stein wrote an extensive analysis of the painters whose work interested her most, in terms of their differing relationships to the objects they painted.[8] She delineated several categories of artists: Matisse and others, who worked "not from immediate contact with the object but from a passionate *emotion* about the object"; those like Renoir, who have "direct relation . . . with the *beauty* of the object"; and those like Braque, who "do not get their inspiration from their direct relation to the object but from their *affection* for the object" (NB-A, 14; my emphasis). Cézanne and Picasso are the only two artists she regarded as "master of the realisation of the object itself": "In none of [the other artists] does the reality of the object count, what I might call the actual earthyness of the object the object for the object's sake. That is the big point of difference" (NB-A, 19; B, 1). In this analysis, she clearly identified her own aesthetic orientation with Cézanne's and Picasso's. Many early critics deplored Cézanne's departures from traditional ideas of beauty and the neutrality of his technique, which subjects landscapes, still lifes, and the human form to the same dispassionate analysis and renders them with the same unifying *facture*. But the terms of Stein's analysis, which clearly oppose the "direct relation to the object" to the mediations of "beauty," "emotion," or "affection," suggest that these violations of conventional expectations contributed to her sense of the immediacy of his presentation of objects.

In *Art and Illusion*, Gombrich quotes from Roland Fréart de Chambray's 1662 treatise, *Idée de perfection de la peinture*, to illustrate how strongly the tradition of illusionistic painting always depended upon rejecting immediate visual sensation in favor of conventional schemata:

> Whenever the painter claims that he imitates things as he sees them he is sure to see them wrongly. . . . Before he takes up his pencil or brush he must therefore adjust his eye to reasoning according to the principles of art which teach how to see things not only as they are in themselves but also how they should be represented. *For it would often be a grave mistake to paint them exactly as the eye sees them, however much this may look like a paradox.*[9]

Gombrich contends that this apparent paradox accounts for the fact that the long tradition of illusionistic art "collapsed as soon as the value of this tradition was questioned by those who relied on the innocent eye."

Courbet, whom Apollinaire and Gleizes and Metzinger later identified as the father of cubism, was the first painter to call himself a "realist." In the words of Castagnary, one of the first champions of French Realist art, "Courbet's great claim is to represent what he sees. It is, in fact, one of his favorite axioms that everything that does not appear upon the retina is outside the domain of painting."[10] Pursuing this new demand for an ever-greater fidelity to direct retinal sensations, the impressionists began to undermine the structural principles of traditional representational painting. But it was Cézanne's work that signaled the crucial break in this tradition. His extreme fidelity to notating his visual sensations, combined with his rigorous attention to pictorial logic, led him to create paintings whose new semiotic structures challenged the most fundamental premises of illusionistic painting and laid the groundwork for both cubism and the nonrepresentational art that followed.

Stein takes this demand for unmediated vision as her major theme in *Picasso* (1938). After describing nineteenth-century painters beginning with Courbet as "preoccupied with their technique which was to express more and more what they were seeing, the seduction of things seen," she presents Picasso as the culmination of this tradition that opposes unmediated "seeing" to conventionalized "knowing" (17). Time and again she insists that, while "the other painters satisfied themselves with the appearance, and always the appearance, which was not at all what they could see but what they knew was there," Picasso paints only what he actually sees. With the extreme partisanship that characterizes all of her later writings on Picasso, she asserts, "With the exception of some African sculpture, no one had ever tried to express things seen not as one knows them but as they are when one sees them without remembering having looked at them" (15). As a historical account of Picasso's contribution to the aesthetics of modernist painting, these claims are as inaccurate as they are extravagant. In fact, the terms of Stein's discussion reveal how strongly her understanding of painting was shaped by the aesthetics of unmediated vision that began to prevail in the mid-nineteenth century and reached its culmination—and its crisis point—in the works of Cézanne.

Stein's opposition between "seeing" and "knowing" echoes John Ruskin's doctrine of the "innocence of the eye," formulated almost a century earlier:

> [W]e always suppose that we *see* what we only know, and have hardly any consciousness of the real aspect of the signs we have learned to interpret. . . .
>
> The perception of solid Form is entirely a matter of experience. We *see* nothing but flat colours; and it is only by a series of experiments that we find out that a stain of black or grey indicates the dark side of a solid substance, or that a feint hue indicates that the object in which it appears is far away. The whole technical power of painting depends on our recovery of what may be called the *innocence of the eye*; that is to say, of a sort of childish perception of these flat stains of colour, merely as such, without consciousness of what they signify,—as a blind man would see them if suddenly gifted with sight.[11]

Written in defense of Turner's painting, Ruskin's description of the nature of unmediated "seeing" precisely anticipated the theoretical premises of the impressionists.

Throughout *Art and Illusion*, Gombrich convincingly argues that the "innocent eye" is a myth, part of the nineteenth-century inductivist ideal that posited the pure observation of uninterpreted fact. Following Karl Popper, he emphasizes that "[e]very observation . . . is a result of a question we ask nature, and every question implies a tentative hypothesis."[12] The demand for an unmediated vision in painting was, itself, shaped by a hypothetical model of perception based on Berkeley's *New Theory of Vision*, which was virtually unchallenged in the nineteenth century. Ruskin's description of what the "innocent eye" sees is based on this model, as were the observations of the impressionists. William James's studies of the process of perception are grounded in the same fundamental hypothesis. Because they shared a common model of perception, the sciences of psychology and optics served to validate the painters' claims that they were rendering the empirical data of immediate retinal sensations. This historical intersection of psychology and painting illuminates the convergence of these two areas of interest in Stein's aesthetic formation.

Although James cautions that a "pure sensation" is an "abstraction never realized in adult life," he too succumbs to the allure of Ruskin's doctrine as a program for painting:

> The whole education of the artist consists in his learning to see the presented signs as well as the represented things. No matter what the field of vision *means*, he sees it also as it *feels*—that is, as a collection of patches of color bounded by lines—the whole forming an optical diagram of whose intrinsic proportions one who is not an artist has hardly a conscious inkling. The ordinary man's attention passes *over* them to their import; the artist's turns back and dwells *upon* them for their own sake. "Don't draw the thing as it *is*, but as it *looks*!" is the endless advice of every teacher to his pupil; forgetting that what it "is" is what it would also "look" provided it were placed in what we have called the "normal" situation for vision. In this situation the sensation as "sign" and the sensation as "object" coalesce into one, and there is no contrast between them.[13]

Throughout *The Principles of Psychology* (1890), James's discussions of visual perception emphasize the gap between the incomplete, fragmentary, or distorted "signs" of immediate retinal sensations and the familiar objects they signify. This semiotic analogy that James derived from Berkeley helps to elucidate more precisely the nature of the challenge that the painters' goal of rendering direct retinal sensations posed to time-honored conventions of representational painting. The impressionists took as their primary object sensations of light striking the retina. In James's terms, their basic unit of signification corresponded not to the "sensation as 'object'" of normalized perception but to the "sensation as 'sign'" (or what Saussurean linguistics would call the signifier). Most radically in Monet's and, later, in Seurat's canvases, a multitude of small patches or dots of color notate the fragmentary signs of direct retinal sensation. This technique shatters the illusory coalescence of signifier and signified object that characterizes both normalized perception and conventional techniques of representing objects in painting and the concomitant illusion of the canvas as a transparent window opening into deep space. The surface design of color patches retards easy recognition of familiar objects and refuses to dissolve into illusory depth. By foregrounding the material patterning of the signifiers that model the raw data of visual sensations, these canvases demand that the viewer work *through* the surface design in order to achieve belated recognition of the objects it signifies.

Before the impressionists, other nineteenth-century painters' efforts to re-create sensations of light and color entailed a similar foregrounding of the painted surface. Both Constable's brushwork and Courbet's use of the palette knife roughened the texture of their canvases, prefiguring the increasingly assertive surface designs of the impressionists and Cézanne. This heightened emphasis on the material reality of the medium, on the "painting . . . —before being a battle-horse, a nude woman, or whatever anecdote—[as] essentially a flat surface covered with colors assembled in a certain order" (to quote Maurice Denis's famous phrase, which first appeared in 1890), was the seemingly paradoxical result of the nineteenth-century painters' ongoing quest for an empirical realism of direct sensation.[14] The more exclusively they concentrated on notating the fragmentary signifiers of color sensations, the more strikingly their canvases foregrounded their surface designs and, consequently, their autonomous reality.

This tension inherent in impressionist painting became even more extreme in the paintings of Cézanne. While he shared his contemporaries' commitment to rendering color sensations, which led the impressionists to flatten depth and dissolve the contours of objects, he was unwilling to sacrifice his equally strong perceptions of depth and the solidity of objects. One of his letters emphasizes the enormous tension between the conflicting demands of these two kinds of sensations: "For improvements in realization, there is only nature, and the eye is trained by contact with it. It becomes concentric by looking and working. I mean that, in an orange, an apple, a ball, a head, there is a culminating point, and this point is always —*in spite of the terrible effect* [*of*] *light and shade, sensations of color*—the closest to our eye; the edges of objects recede in relation to a center placed in our horizon."[15] Monet and Seurat focused exclusively on one kind of "sensation as 'sign,'" which Ruskin described as "flat stains of colors." Not satisfied with notating only these sensations and ignoring all the rest, Cézanne attempted to render the various and sometimes mutually contradictory sensory signs that combine to form the complex object of visual perception. His method of reconciling these conflicting visual signs resulted in paintings that manifest a greater tension between material surface and illusory depth and, consequently, a more direct challenge to the tradition of Western representational painting than the work of the impressionists.

Stein's years of study with William James enabled her to understand the striking "distortions" in Cézanne's paintings as faithful models of the multiple and fragmentary signs of immediate visual sensations. One of James's illustrations of the vast difference between direct sensations and acquired perceptions could serve as an accurate description of some of Cézanne's characteristic deformations of the familiar shapes of objects:

> So when I get, as now, a brown eye-picture with lines not
> parallel, and with angles unlike, and call it my big solid rec-
> tangular walnut library-table, that picture is not the table. It is
> not even like the table as the table is for vision, when rightly
> seen. It is a distorted perspective view of three of the sides of
> what I mentally *perceive* (more or less) in its totality and un-
> distorted shape. (*Principles of Psychology*, 2:78)

James's "brown eye-picture" aptly describes the tables rendered in
Cézanne's famous *Portrait of Gustave Geffroy* (1895), *The Kitch-
en Table* (1880–90), and many other still lifes, with their "lines not
parallel, and with angles unlike." In this passage, as in many others
in *The Principles of Psychology*, James goes on to emphasize that
each completed perception is a complex mental object, composed
of "reproduced sights and contacts tied together with the present
sensation in the unity of a thing with a name," far removed from the
immediate visual signs that it transforms into a familiar object.

"As regards shape," James observes, "almost all the retinal
shapes that objects throw are perspective 'distortions.' Square
table-tops constantly present two acute and two obtuse angles;
circles drawn on our wallpapers, our carpets, or on sheets of paper,
usually show like ellipses; parallels approach as they recede; human bodies are foreshortened; *and the transitions from one to
another of these altering forms are infinite and continual*" (2:238–
39; my emphasis). Cézanne not only "distorted" the shapes of
objects to correspond to the kinds of "retinal shapes" James describes; he also employed a number of techniques, including *passage* and multiple outlines, to suggest the accumulation of visual
data—the minute transitions and tiny readjustments—that contributes to the process of perception. Instead of being modeled
according to conventional chiaroscuro, the objects in Cézanne's
paintings are frequently bounded by a number of outlines of strikingly different tonalities. A letter he wrote from Estaque in 1876
strongly suggests that this rejection of chiaroscuro modeling was
grounded in his scrupulous observation of nature: "The sun is so
terrific here that it seems to me as if the objects are silhouetted not
only in black and white, but in blue, red, brown, violet. I may be

mistaken, but it seems that this is the opposite of modeling."[16] Later he had no doubts: "We should not say model, we should say *modulate*."[17]

It was this strategy of notating everything, including volume and depth, in terms of colors juxtaposed without transitional tones, that posed the most serious challenge to the fundamental conventions of illusionistic painting. Many of Cézanne's early critics regarded this as the most striking evidence of his gaucherie, but most recent art historians acknowledge how powerfully these techniques "contribute . . . to the impression of an emerging order, of an object in the act of appearing, organizing itself before our eyes," in Merleau-Ponty's words.[18]

Although it is important to emphasize how strongly Cézanne's innovative techniques were grounded in his meticulous analysis of the process of visual perception, it would be a mistake to regard his art as naïve naturalism, the simple transcription of raw sensation onto canvas. Cézanne's dicta reveal how conscious he was that his was not an "innocent eye," that his observations were always mediated by his awareness of the concrete resources of his medium. He describes this mediated vision as "reading nature, that is, seeing it through the veil of interpretation in terms of color patches that succeed one another according to the law of harmony."[19] He frequently emphasized that his work was not a naïve "copy" of nature but a relational model that "represents" it in terms of the material he has at his disposal: "I wished to copy nature. I could not. But I was satisfied when I had discovered that the sun, for instance, could not be *reproduced*, but that it must be *represented* by something else . . . by color."[20] Despite, or perhaps more accurately, because of the intensity of his commitment to "realizing" his sensations, Cézanne was always aware that seeing was "reading," through a grid determined by the concrete resources of his medium, and that the colored patches he arranged on his canvases were signs, not replicas, of the objects of perception.

What he called the "logic of organized sensations" dictated the composition of his canvases. Cézanne's paintings present a dense pattern of color and texture, in which the clearly visible *facture* serves both to encode the signs of visual sensation and to create a self-sufficient surface design. Maurice Denis, Cézanne's most acute early critic, called attention to the inevitable foregrounding of the surface plane that results from the painter's precise rendering of the "exigencies of the eye": "The entire canvas is a tapestry where each color plays separately and yet mixes [*confond*] its sonority in the ensemble. The characteristic aspect of Cézanne's canvases comes from this juxtaposition, this mosaic of tones, separated and lightly grounded in one another."[21]

Like the tiny daubs of paint that served as the basic compositional elements of impressionist paintings, the larger patches of color in Cézanne's canvases break the traditional illusory coalescence of signifier and object signified. Each of the colored dots in a Manet painting can be read as notating a single "sensation as 'sign.'" While some of the color patches in Cézanne's paintings function similarly, many do not, individually, signify anything. As Lawrence Gowing has observed, "It is the relationships between them—relationships of affinity and contrast, the progressions from tone to tone in a color scale, and the modulations from scale to scale—that parallel the apprehension of the world."[22]

In "Cézanne and the Unity of Modern Art," Clement Greenberg argues that Cézanne's efforts to relate "every part of the illusion in depth to a surface pattern endowed with equally valid aesthetic rights" resulted in unified surface designs that "led straight, in an interval of only five or six years after his death, to a kind of painting as flat as any the West has seen since the Middle Ages"— the cubism of Picasso and Braque.[23] Greenberg's account of what he calls the "involuntary break with the Renaissance tradition" begun by Manet and completed by Cézanne focuses exclusively on the issue of their "inadvertent emphasis on the flat plane." What I have attempted to show is that this foregrounding of the surface plane, far from inadvertent, was the inevitable result of the commitment to rendering the multiple and fragmentary data that contribute to the process of perception, instead of the already constituted objects of normalized appearances. It was this shift of focus, which necessarily entailed a heightened emphasis on the material patterning of paint on canvas, that revolutionized the semiotic structure of painting.

In "A Transatlantic Interview 1946," Stein described the "new feeling about composition" that she derived from Cézanne's paintings in terms of a similar—and equally radical—reformulation of the premises and methods of literary realism: "It was not solely the realism of the characters but the realism of the composition which was the important thing, the realism of the composition of my thoughts" (16). Earlier in the interview, Stein discussed the impact of Cézanne's new sense of composition on her writing in more detail:

> Up to that time composition had consisted of a central idea, to which everything else was an accompaniment and separate but was not an end in itself, and Cézanne conceived the idea that in composition one thing was as important as another thing. Each part is as important as the whole, and that impressed me enormously, and it impressed me so much that I began to write *Three Lives* under this influence and this idea of composition and I was more interested in composition at that moment, *this background of word-system*, which had come to me from this reading I had done. I was obsessed by this idea of composition, and the Negro story ("Melanctha" in *Three Lives*) was the quintessence of it. (TI, 15; my emphasis)

No longer subordinated to the organization of ideas, Stein's "background of word-system" comes to the fore as the predominant element of the composition. Cézanne's surface designs were conceived in an effort to create a perfect match between the concrete signifiers of painting and the empirical data of perception. And, like Cézanne's "veil" of "color patches that succeed one another according to the law of harmony," Stein's foregrounded "word-system" creates a new mode of realism that inheres in the material patterning of the composition, not merely re-presentng the objects of completed conception but modeling the processes of perception and cognition. As she defines it here, it is a "realism of the composition" that is the formal embodiment of the "composition of [her] thoughts."

The Jamesian model of consciousness suggests that this new mode of realism, grounded in the processes of perception and cognition, would necessarily pose as great a challenge to the conventional language of fiction as it did to traditional techniques of representation in painting. Although James regarded language as an inextricable part of what he called the "stream of consciousness," one of the major themes of *The Principles of Psychology* is the extent to which conventional "language works against our perception of the truth" (1:241). The "truth" he is discussing in this passage is what he calls the "actual concrete consciousness of man." James observes that we tend to label our experiences with names that fail to register the complexity of the process of apprehension: "We name our thoughts simply, each after its thing, as if each knew its own thing and nothing else."

In his discussion of the "stream of consciousness," James again laments the inadequacy of language as an instrument for registering the operations of consciousness (1:243–46). The difficulty, as he sees it, lies not in naming the "substantive conclusions" of thought but in registering what he calls the "transitive parts" of the "stream of consciousness," the "thoughts of relations" that "lead us from one substantive conclusion to the next." Significantly, James locates the problem in our habits of apprehending language, not in a lack of semantic resources within the system itself: "[I]nstead of catching the feeling of relation moving to its term, we find we have caught some substantive thing, usually the last word we were pronouncing, statically taken, and with its function, tendency, and particular meaning in the sentence quite evaporated." The "transitive parts" of speech can express these relations, but we habitually fail to pay attention to them:

> There is not a conjunction or a preposition, and hardly an adverbial phrase, syntactic form, or inflection of voice, in human speech, that does not express some shading or other of relation which we at some moment actually feel to exist between the larger objects of our thought. . . . We ought to say a feeling of *and*, a feeling of *if*, a feeling of *but*, and a feeling of *by*, quite as readily as we say a feeling of *blue* or a feeling of *cold*. Yet we do not: so inveterate has our habit become of recognizing the existence of the substantive parts alone, that language almost re-

fuses to lend itself to any other use. . . . All *dumb* or anonymous psychic states have, owing to this error, been coolly
suppressed; or, if recognized at all, have been named after the
substantive perception they led to, as thoughts "about" this
object or "about" that, the stolid word *about* engulfing all
their delicate idiosyncracies in its monotonous sound.

Implicit in this passage and elsewhere in James's writings is the assumption that language has the semantic resources to register the
movements of consciousness—a belief Stein shared during the early
years of her career.

But as Valéry has observed, "The essence of prose is to perish
—that is, to be 'understood'—that is, to be dissolved, destroyed
without return, entirely replaced by the image or impulse that
it conveys according to the conventions of language."[24] What
James's discussion suggests is that if a text is to render the "delicate
idiosyncracies" of thought it must disrupt conventional reading
practices by presenting a stylistic surface that resists this tendency
to dissolve into "thoughts 'about' this object or 'about' that." More
specifically, James's comments imply, it must distort conventional
syntax in order to call attention to the connective elements of language that express what he calls "thoughts of relations." The texture of the prose must be roughened, the utterance must be made
less "transparent," because the reader must be forced to experience
the language word by word, as an embodiment of process, not
merely as a means to a conclusion. Inevitably, the more strenuously
a text resists this habitual tendency to dissolve into familiar images
of the human and social world, the more forcefully the patterning
of its language will assert itself as the primary reality.

Victor Shklovsky was the first literary theoretician to suggest
that this would be the necessary consequence of every demand for
perceptual realism in art. Shklovsky's doctrine of defamiliarization
has a particular historical interest in relation to Stein's writings because of the similarity in their artistic and intellectual points of reference. His 1917 essay "Art as Technique" was produced in the
contexts of Russian futurism, which was closely allied to French
avant-garde art before World War I, and Jamesian psychology. In

it, Shklovsky asserts as an aesthetic absolute the idea, which in fact came to the fore only in the second half of the nineteenth century, that the "purpose of art is to impart the sensations of things as they are perceived and not as they are known." What follows from this assumption is his famous prescription: "The technique of art is to make objects 'unfamiliar,' to make forms difficult, to increase the difficulty and length of perception because the process of perception is an aesthetic end in itself and must be prolonged. Art is a means of re-experiencing the making of objects, but objects already made have no importance for art."[25] The provocative sentence that concludes this passage squarely confronts the consequences of this shift of focus from the signified object to the material patterning of signifiers that models the process of perception by de-automatizing conventional forms. What Shklovsky suggests is that the art object that results from this program inevitably flaunts its own artfulness, its irreducible difference from the "real" object that served as its point of departure.

In literature as in painting, this increasing demand for a faithful re-creation of the actual processes of perception and cognition necessarily entailed radical deviations from conventional forms of verisimilitude, as Shklovsky's doctrine suggests. "A novel is a mirror that walks along a highway [*un roman est un miroir qui se promène sur une grande route*]."[26] Stendhal's metaphor, with its eerie absence of human agency, succinctly conveys the ideal of classic realist fiction: a verbal surface that dissolves into a pure, neutral reproduction of social reality. Zola borrows the classic metaphor for illusionistic painting to propose the same ideal transparency: "The realist screen is a simple window-pane, very thin, very clear, which aspires to be so perfectly transparent that images pass through it and reproduce themselves in [all] their reality."[27] Elsewhere, Zola uses an auditory metaphor to suggest a similar equivalence between the medium and the objects it represents: the novelist "listens to nature and writes according to its dictation."[28] This formulation echoes Balzac's famous characterization of his role as the "secretary" of French society, merely transcribing the history it dictates.[29]

Roland Barthes has suggested that what defines realism is not the origin of the model it purports to copy but the exteriority of its models to language.[30] Indeed, all of these canonical metaphors for the realist text assume a reality that is simply *there*, prior to and exterior to the language that reproduces it. And they all emphasize the extent to which the classic realist novel is or, more accurately, pretends to be unconscious of its literariness. While both the visual and the auditory metaphors propose an ideal correspondence between the medium and the objects it represents, they equally ignore the vast difference between the realm of discourse and the external world the novel purports to reflect.

The new mode of realism Stein began to create in *Three Lives* is grounded in a fundamentally different valuation of language. With her shift of focus from the "realism of character" to the "realism of the composition of . . . thoughts," language, like Cézanne's patches of color, becomes a property shared, at least to some extent, by the object and the medium. Of course, quoted speech and thought have always been important components of realist narrative—a fact that Barthes's formulation ignores. But before the twentieth century, with very few exceptions, characters' thoughts, like their speeches, were presented in language that conformed to the norms of the narrative discourse. Interior speech and narrated monologue served more to report the results of thought than to trace its process. Stein's project of modeling the actual "composition" of thought in language necessarily entailed not only disrupting this normative discourse but also challenging its authority to represent the reality of human consciousness.

Stein was not the first—or the last—writer whose efforts to model what William James called the "actual concrete consciousness of man" resulted in compositions that flaunt the artfulness of their elaborately patterned language. In "A Transatlantic Interview 1946," Stein acknowledged that she had recognized in the prose of Henry James and Flaubert "a little" of the same "new feeling about composition" that she saw in Cézanne's paintings (16). Henry James's labyrinthine sentences create a verbal surface that strenuously resists the reader's habitual rush to conclusions in order to register the subtle intricacies of the thought processes of his characters. Proust credited Flaubert with an "entirely new and personal usage" of tenses, past participles, and certain prepositions and pronouns, which "has renewed our vision of things almost as much as Kant, with his Categories, the theories of Knowledge and Reality of the exterior world."[31] But already in *Three Lives* Stein's manipulations of syntax, sound, and rhythm are more radical than James's and more systematic than Flaubert's. The following chapter will focus on the ambivalent status of language in this text, Stein's first effort to create a new mode of realism analogous to Cézanne's.

*Three Lives*: The Realism of the Composition

N *The Autobiography of Alice B. Toklas* Stein
recalled that she wrote *Three Lives* while "looking and looking" at
Cézanne's *Portrait of Mme Cézanne* (ABT, 34). Before she began
these stories in 1905, she had written three narratives: *Q.E.D.*,
a semiautobiographical account of a lesbian triangle; *Fernhurst*;
and five chapters of a family chronicle, which later served as the
beginning of *The Making of Americans*. Compared to *Three Lives*
and the texts that followed, these are conventional narratives, except for the theme of lesbianism that appears in *Q.E.D. Three
Lives*, and especially the story "Melanctha," which recasts *Q.E.D.*
in a different social and racial milieu and a new idiom, reveals how
radically Stein transformed her style in response to her initial confrontation with modernist painting.

Flaubert's "Un Coeur simple" was the literary point of depar-
ture for her first attempt to create a mode of realism analogous to
Cézanne's in her own medium. In 1905 she began translating "Un
Coeur simple" into English. She soon abandoned this project to
write "The Good Anna," her own story of the life of a simple
servant woman. After completing it, she went on to write "The
Gentle Lena" and "Melanctha" and named the collection of stories
*Three Lives* (originally *Three Histories*, in deliberate homage to
Flaubert's *Trois Contes*).[1]

"Un Coeur simple" provided Stein with both a subject and a
structural model for "The Good Anna," the first story in which she
began to explore this new principle of composition. Stein's Anna,
like Flaubert's Félicité, is a hardworking servant, totally devoted to
her employers; her own quiet existence, like Félicité's, is shaped by
events in other people's lives. Flaubert's story narrates Félicité's un-
eventful life from her adolescence to her death. Its episodic narrative structure demonstrates a high degree of temporal and logical

discontinuity. "The Good Anna" is an equally discontinuous episodic narrative, which recounts the life span of its heroine from
childhood to death. Flaubert's unemphatic narrative unfolds the
repeated pattern of Félicité's ardent loves and losses—her lover,
her mistress's daughter, her own nephew, and, finally, her beloved
parrot—which culminates in her epiphanic deathbed vision of the
parrot as the Holy Ghost. "The Good Anna" lacks this kind of
unifying pattern, but Stein's story makes deliberate use of some
of the other narrative strategies Flaubert employed in "Un Coeur
simple." His text frequently juxtaposes short, even one-sentence
paragraphs to create a slight discontinuity of action:

> Elle eut envie de se mettre dans les demoiselles de la Vi-
> erge. Mme Aubain l'en dissuada.
> Un événement considérable surgit: le mariage de Paul.[2]
>
> [She wanted to join the ladies of the Virgin. Mme Aubain
> talked her out of it.
> An important event suddenly emerged: the marriage of
> Paul.]

The "événement considérable" is merely reported in passing, not
described. Stein makes similar use of short, unemphatic paragraphs
to recount the events in Anna's life:

> The wedding day grew always nearer. At last it came and
> went. (TL, 33)

The wedding of her mistress's daughter changes Anna's life, forc-
ing her to find a new employer; like the marriage in "Un Coeur
simple," it is merely noted in a short paragraph. For both of these
servant women, the kinds of major events that shape the plots of
conventional novels take place only in other people's lives, yet they
have considerable effects on their own situations. Character is em-
phatically not destiny for these women. Because of their social position, the course of their lives is the by-product of the actions of
others. Appropriately, their stories lack the strong sense of narrative causality that shapes traditional fiction.

Stein's Anna is a far more voluble character than Flaubert's Félicité. This difference indicates a major divergence between Stein's project and the literary model that served as her point of departure. While Félicité's speech is never quoted and only rarely reported, Stein eagerly embraced the challenge of creating speeches for characters whose command of standard English is limited. Both Anna and the characters in "The Gentle Lena," the second story she wrote for *Three Lives*, are German immigrants. "Melanctha," the third story, is set in a southern black community.

Paradoxically, the more accurately dialectal speech is rendered in fiction, the more insistently it calls attention to itself as linguistic artifice. The more radically language deviates from the norms of conventional narrative discourse to reproduce actual dialect features, the more insistently it resists the normal tendency of prose to "dissolve" easily into meaning. In *Three Lives* Stein avoided phonetic approximations of dialectal pronunciation, but she systematically used syntactical deformation and repetition to create stylized models of the dialectal speech patterns of her characters. In the first story Anna's speeches are frequently introduced by descriptions that call attention to their abrupt, jerky rhythms:

> "Miss Mary," Anna began. She had stopped just within the door, her body and her face stiff with repression, her teeth closed hard and the white lights flashing sharply in the pale, clean blue of her eyes. Her bearing was full of the strange coquetry of anger and of fear, the stiffness, the bridling, the suggestive movement underneath the rigidity of forced control, all the queer ways the passions have to show themselves all one.
>
> "Miss Mary," the words came slowly with thick utterance and with jerks, but always firm and strong. "Miss Mary, I can't stand it any more like this. When you tell me anything to do, I do it. I do everything I can and you know I work myself sick for you. The blue dressings in your room makes too much work to have for summer. Miss Jane don't know what work is. If you want to do things like that I go away."
>
> Anna stopped still. Her words had not the strength of meaning they were meant to have, but the power in the mood

of Anna's soul frightened and awed Miss Mary through and through. (29)

Her short, simple sentences, filled with grammatical errors, "had not the strength of meaning they were meant to have." Consequently, in this passage and elsewhere in the story, the narrator surrounds Anna's quoted speech with descriptions and interpretations of her body language, which emphasize the inadequacy of her language to her emotions. In contrast to Anna, Mrs. Lehntman, who is called upon to help Anna speak to her mistress in this scene, speaks "slowly" and more fluently than her friend (43). The rhythm of her long polysyndetic sentences is markedly different from Anna's "sharp and short" utterances in the preceding passage:

> "Miss Wadsmith, Anna feels how good and kind you are, and she talks about it all the time, and what you do for her in every way you can, and she is very grateful and never would want to go away from you, only she thinks it would be better now that Mrs. Goldthwaite has this big new house and will want to manage it in her own way, she thinks perhaps it would be better if Mrs. Goldthwaite had all new servants with her to begin with, and not a girl like Anna who knew her when she was a little girl." (35)

This story simply presents Anna's difficulty with language as a naturalistic character trait. The next two stories Stein wrote explore more extensively the role of language in shaping the thoughts and the lives of characters whose imperfect command of English makes self-expression an arduous labor. By dramatizing these linguistic struggles, the stories in *Three Lives* foreground the material reality of language as an arbitrary and problematic system, far from a transparent medium of communication.

In *The Colloquial Style in America*, Richard Bridgman has observed that in nineteenth-century American fiction dialectal speech was generally confined to a "special arena fenced in by quotation marks," sharply contrasting with the normative narrative voice, except in a few first-person narratives like the *Adventures of Huckleberry Finn*.[3] In *Three Lives* the use of immigrant characters motivates the syntactical deformation that breaks their speech into unusual and assertive rhythmic patterns, but these stylistic effects overflow the restricted area bounded by quotation marks to pervade the entire narrative. Dorrit Cohn uses the rather infelicitous term "stylistic contagion," borrowed from Leo Spitzer, to describe the encroachment of a character's speech style into the surrounding discourse; Hugh Kenner, in *Joyce's Voices*, more jocularly calls it the "Uncle Charles principle."[4] The style of "The Good Anna" is strangely mixed. It frequently approaches the simple diction and awkward syntax of the characters, but it also incorporates words like "coquetry" and "repression" (in the passage cited above) that are far removed from their lexicon and, consequently, from their mental horizons as well. In the subsequent stories Stein wrote for *Three Lives*, she sharply limited her lexicon to create a narrative idiom that closely approximates the speech of the characters. This assertive, evenly textured verbal surface is analogous to the surfaces of Cézanne's canvases, with their dense patterning of brushstrokes that unite objects and background in a tapesty of color patches of equal value.

Again, Flaubert can be seen as a literary model for compositional principles similar to those suggested by Cézanne's painting. Proust described reading Flaubert as undertaking a "continuous, monstrous, dreary, indefinite march" on the "great moving sidewalk" of his prose. For Proust, the beauty of Flaubert's style, which he greatly admired, was grammatical; it derived, in part, from the powerful and original rhythms created by his "deforming syntax" (*syntaxe déformante*).[5] One of Flaubert's most striking innovations, which often motivates his peculiar manipulation of syntax, is the use of free indirect discourse that pervades most of his texts. This third-person, past-tense rendering of speech or thought which approaches the verbal style of a character allows for almost imperceptible shifts in and out of a character's point of view. It creates an even stylistic surface that approaches the structure of oral speech while it remains a distinctly "written" style. For Flaubert, the *mot juste* can be the word or phrase that is slightly wrong—flat or awkward, according to correct literary usage, but exactly the right word to approximate the sensibility of his characters.

Henry James provides an American model for a narrative discourse that incorporates traces of the rhythms of colloquial speech and thought. Although Stein always claimed not to have read James seriously until much later in her career, *Q.E.D.*, one of her earliest narratives, suggests a recent and thoughtful reading of James. It is a limited third-person narrative, with a heroine who functions as a Jamesian central intelligence. Bridgman has argued that Stein's style in this early text owes much to James's example, especially in its use of repetition to create the effect of colloquial speech.[6] James's dislocations of syntax render the fastidious mental discriminations and reevaluations of his eminently conscious characters. But *Q.E.D.* demonstrates nothing of James's technical virtuosity in registering subtle movements of consciousness through rapid alternations of psychonarrative, narrated monologue, and direct quotation of interior speech.[7] Stein did not begin the use of syntactical deformation to model the process of thought until she wrote *Three Lives*.

While James generally preferred to focus on highly articulate characters with finely tuned moral sensibilities, Flaubert was fascinated by stupidity. In the *Dictionnaire des idées reçues* and in many of his narratives as well, he lovingly and ruthlessly exposed the linguistic and mental limitations of commonplace minds, the products of middle-class culture. In "Un Coeur simple," however, he protects the simple Félicité from the corrosive effects of his irony by denying her a voice.[8] In *Three Lives*, Stein extends the narrative strategies of Flaubert and James into a territory they shrank from exploring—the narrowly restricted linguistic universe that confines the speech and thoughts of simple uneducated characters. In "The Gentle Lena" and "Melanctha," to a far greater degree than in the first story, the characters' speeches dominate the narratives, while anecdotal actions and circumstantial details, such as physical descriptions of characters and settings, are reduced to a minimum. In "The Gentle Lena," Stein began to combine direct quotation with extensive use of narrated monologue, Flaubert's favorite device for blurring the distinction between the characters' speech and the narrative voice. In the second and third stories of *Three Lives*, there is

no escape from the linguistic and conceptual boundaries that re-
strict the characters' expression and their thought.

In "The Gentle Lena," the central character suffers as a result
of her linguistic inadequacy. A recent immigrant from Germany
with a limited command of English, she lacks the resources to
defend herself adequately against the verbal barrages to which she
is constantly subjected. Consequently, she becomes the passive vic-
tim of the desires, and the discourse, of others. Her aunt arranges
a marriage for her, which neither she nor the prospective husband
desires, but Lena can never voice her feelings: "Mrs. Haydon spoke
to Lena about it very often. Lena never answered anything at all"
(252). When Mrs. Haydon finally forces her to speak, her words reveal her linguistic helplessness, her total subjugation to the discourse that dominates her:

> "Why, I do anything you say, Aunt Mathilda. Yes, I like
> him. He don't say much to me, but I guess he is a good man,
> and I do anything you say for me to do."
>
> "Well then Lena, why you stand there so silly all the time
> and not answer when I asked you?"
>
> "I didn't hear you say you wanted I should say anything
> to you. I didn't know you wanted me to say nothing. I do what-
> ever you tell me it's right for me to do. I marry Herman Kreder,
> if you want me." (253)

Mrs. Haydon, the German cook, and Lena's friend Mary all scold
her repeatedly and at length, and the reluctant bridegroom's family
subject him to similar verbal assaults. In this masterful series of
long harangues, which combine narrated monologue with quoted
speech, these characters unconsciously reveal the self-absorption
that motivates their manipulation of Lena and Herman:

> Did Lena think it gave Mrs. Haydon any pleasure, to work so
> hard to make Lena happy, and get her a good husband, and
> then Lena was so thankless and never did anything that any-
> body wanted. It was a lesson to poor Mrs. Haydon not to do
> things any more for anybody. Let everybody take care of them-

selves and never come to her with any troubles; she knew better now than to meddle to make other people happy. It just made trouble for her and her husband did not like it. He always said she was too good, and nobody ever thanked her for it, and there Lena was always standing stupid and not answering anything anybody wanted. Lena could always talk enough to those silly girls she liked so much, and always sat with, but who never did anything for her except to take away her money, and here was her aunt who tried so hard and was so good to her and treated her just like one of her own children and Lena stood there, and never made any answer and never tried to please her aunt, or to do anything that her aunt wanted. "No, it ain't no use your standin' there and cryin', now, Lena. Its too late now to care about that Herman. You should have cared some before, and then you wouldn't have to stand and cry now, and be a disappointment to me, and then I get scolded by my husband for taking care of everybody, and nobody ever thankful." (256)

Mrs. Haydon herself is unaware of the persistent contradictions between her professed concern for her niece's happiness and her outrage at the girl's passive resistance to her own plans. Her syntax, which loosely strings together short phrases with a plethora of coordinating conjunctions, clearly reveals to the reader the tenuous logic of her thought processes. The syntax and movement of this passage typify the way these voluble characters entangle themselves in webs of contradictions each time they berate the young people. Their repetition of the same judgmental words heightens the reader's awareness of language as an instrument of culture, enforcing the dominant values of a community. Both Lena and Herman tacitly reject the conventional wisdom that marriage always leads to happiness, but both are unable to articulate their reasons for opposing this social norm. Lena's only defense is silence, while Herman finally takes action by running away. After this, Mrs. Haydon calls Lena "stupid" to have lost him; the cook says it is Herman who is "stupid," and, on the following page, Mary calls Lena "stupid to be sorry" to have lost him (257, 259, 260). "Stupid," "disgrace" and other judgmental words are the blunt instruments of culture which, with their repeated blows, finally force the couple to submit to marriage.

After their capitulation, Herman adapts better to marriage than Lena does. For her, marriage and children only increase her isolation and alienation. As she silently succumbs to total passivity, "gentle," the adjective used repeatedly to characterize her earlier in the story, is replaced by "lifeless." Finally Lena dies in childbirth:

> When the baby was come out at last, it was like its mother lifeless. While it was coming, Lena had grown very pale and sicker. When it was all over Lena had died, too, and nobody knew just how it had happened to her. (279)

The discourse effectively blurs the moment of passage from figurative to literal lifelessness. This bitter play on words is an appropriate conclusion for this powerful story of victimization by language and the social conventions it enforces.

When Samuel Beckett staked out "impotence, ignorance" as his artistic terrain, in contrast to Joyce's exuberant linguistic virtuosity, he believed he was the first to embrace that project: "I don't think impotence has been exploited in the past."[9] Apparently he was not acquainted with *Three Lives*, in which Stein used the verbal impotence of her characters, combined with a similarly restricted narrative idiom, to create a poetics of impotence, of antieloquence. More systematically than the first two stories she wrote for *Three Lives*, "Melanctha" probes the ways in which the confines of her characters' language shape and, finally, impede their understanding. The central incident in "Melanctha" recasts her 1903 novella *Q.E.D.*, a story of "college bred American women of the wealthier class," in the vastly different social and linguistic world of a southern black community (QED, 54). Stein considered "Melanctha" the "quintessence" of the new compositional principles she developed in response to the work of Flaubert and Cézanne (TI, 15). A comparison of these two texts, written only three years apart, reveals how consciously she reevaluated the resources of her medium and how radically she transformed her narrative strategies in response to the twin challenges posed by the work of Cézanne and Flaubert.

The longest and most polished of the three works Stein wrote before *Three Lives*, *Q.E.D.* retraces the course of her own passionate and ultimately painful involvement with May Bookstaver, a fellow student at Johns Hopkins, from its tentative beginnings to her final realization of its hopelessness.[10] Apparently Stein wrote *Q.E.D.* purely for herself, as an effort to understand her own recent and painful experience. Adele, its heroine, is a resolutely rational character, committed to verbal "analysis" and "dissection" of her experience (QED, 72, 82). Her first speech announces this fundamental personality trait: "I am reasonable because I know the difference between understanding and not understanding and I am just because I have no opinion about things I don't understand" (56). Her intense attraction to Helen soon threatens the placidity of her "reasonableness" and forces her to deal with things she doesn't understand. Challenging her naïve faith that "all morality [is] so easily reducible to formula," her passion for Helen forces her to confront not only the question of lesbianism but also the problem of Helen's prior involvement with Mable (93). Her gradual realization that Mabel is supporting Helen further intensifies the moral complexity of her situation.

*Q.E.D.* focuses on Adele's successive efforts to control her moral and emotional confusion by analyzing it in dialogues, letters, and interior monologues. According to Adele, the major obstacle that ultimately separates her from Helen is not Mabel but irreconcilable differences of temperament. "Their pulses were differently timed" (104); Helen's "courage," her emotional spontaneity, is out of sync with the slower, more "cowardly" nature of Adele's responses, which stems from her need for intellectual and moral clarity. These differences make the "long struggle" between them as "inevitable as their separate natures" (92). Her lover, who resents being subjected to Adele's constant verbal analysis, perceives her resolute rationality as a barrier to emotional intensity: "Haven't you ever stopped thinking long enough to feel?" (66). The force of her passions temporarily overrides her habitual rational controls, and she lets herself feel and accept her love for Helen, with all its painful moral ambiguities. But by this time it is too late; their different rhythms of response have thwarted the possibility of union. Before the end of the novel, Adele has regained her habitual intellectual detachment, which allows her to enjoy observing the "working of the machinery" of their schematically opposed personalities as it grinds inexorably to the final impasse (121).

"Melanctha" transforms this narrative material into the story of a heterosexual love affair set in a black community, retaining not only the fundamental personality traits of the two lovers and the course of their passions but the specific content of many passages of dialogue and meditation as well. Adele becomes Jeff Campbell, a "negro" doctor, and Helen is re-created as Melanctha, a mulatto woman. The role of Mabel is split among three characters. Jane Harden initiates Melanctha into the "wisdom" of sexual passion and later reveals Melanctha's prior sexual experience to Jeff. After her affair with Jeff is over, Melanctha's affections are dominated by Jem Richards, her lover, and Rose Johnson, her friend. Leon Katz regards Stein's transformation of *Q.E.D.*'s thinly disguised autobiographical materials into "Melanctha" as a "mode of conceal-ment . . . done originally for psychological rather than aesthetic reasons."[11] Indeed, recasting Adele as a male character displaces the issue of lesbianism, taboo as a literary subject during Stein's life-time, from the center of the narrative, although a trace of it still sur-vives in Melanctha's relationship with Jane. But the other major differences between the two texts, especially the crucial change in social milieu that justifies the radical transformation of language in "Melanctha," clearly reveal the predominance of the new aesthetic concerns Stein had begun to explore in the first two stories of *Three Lives*. In conformity with the episodic narrative structures of "The Good Anna" and "The Gentle Lena," in "Melanctha" the material adapted from *Q.E.D.* becomes the central incident in a story that expands to encompass the heroine's life span from childhood to her early death. In the earlier text, the three women leave New York to travel around Europe. "Melanctha" eliminates these geographical movements, which are largely irrelevant to the dramatic interactions among the characters, and, with them, the kind of concrete descriptive details that create an illusion of circumstantial realism in *Q.E.D.* The realism of the later text inheres in the speeches and thoughts that constitute the essential action of the story.

Recasting *Q.E.D.* in the "negro" community of "Bridgeport" posed the challenge of creating a character who, like Adele and originally Stein herself, needs to "have it all clear out in words always, what everybody is always feeling," but lacks the verbal and conceptual resources provided by their class and educational background (TL, 171). Adele's mind works incessantly to impose rational order on her experiences by formulating them "in definite words" (QED, 64). "All I want to do is to meditate endlessly and think and talk," she confesses to Helen (80). Adele regards language as an infallible instrument for clarifying complex emotional and moral issues. For the characters in "Melanctha," language is, itself, part of the problem. Both Jeff and Melanctha are painfully aware of the inadequacy of their language. During one of their first conversations, Melanctha accuses Jeff, "You don't know very well yourself, what you mean, when you are talking" (TL, 118). Jeff feels the same uncertainty about the efficacy of their communication: "I certainly do wonder, Miss Melanctha, if we know at all really what each other means by what we are always saying" (128).

This sense of the limitations of language is already present as an undercurrent of irony in *Q.E.D.*, which pits Adele's garrulous nature against Helen's silences. From the beginning of their relationship, Adele's words reverberate hollowly out of emotional depths that cannot—or dare not—be named. At the first stirring of these new feelings, "somehow the silence now subtly suggested the significance of their being alone together" (58). Silence, subtle suggestions, a significance that remains forever unarticulated—these are the necessary conditions of the passions Stein explores in *Q.E.D.*, written long before lesbian love entered the accepted discourse of our culture. Immersed in a relationship necessarily governed by a "convention of silence," Adele uses her verbal arsenal to evade or deny her most profound emotions (77). By the time she finally succumbs to her deepest feelings and "learn[s] to stop thinking," she has already lost Helen (86). The last interview between them shows Adele once more in complete command of her verbal resources—and, ironically, in full retreat from the significance of the emotional experiences she has undergone during the course of the narrative. She accuses Helen of hiding behind her silences, while the force of the text, for the reader, has been to reveal how much is hidden by her own customary verbosity. And her ringing affirmation, "Nothing is too good or too holy for clear thinking and definite expression," utterly denies the validity of her unspeakable— yet utterly real—emotional engagement with Helen (132).[12]

Thematically, *Q.E.D.* marks the beginning of Stein's long career of testing the limits of language, but its narrative discourse is still cast entirely in the rational, analytical language of its central character, which it ironizes and punctuates with silences but does not otherwise surpass. "Melanctha" is the first of many texts in which Stein challenges the dominant cultural discourse stylistically as well as thematically. Even more deliberately than in the other stories in *Three Lives,* in "Melanctha" the characters' distance from mainstream American culture is used to motivate a systematic stylistic demonstration of the limits of rational discourse as a medium for interpersonal communication.

In *Q.E.D.,* Adele's linguistic and conceptual system provides her with pat labels to classify her experience. She relies heavily on abstract nouns arranged in sets of binary oppositions: virtues and vices, cowardice and heroism, humility and arrogance. In "Melanctha," Jeff shares Adele's need for conceptual order, but his more restricted lexicon does not include the abstract conceptual terms that dominate Adele's discourse. His speeches consistently translate Adele's abstract nouns into gerundial forms: "heroism" becomes "being game and not hollering"; "passion" is translated into "getting excited"; "living regular" replaces "the middle-class ideal." These changes involve more than a shift to a more colloquial level of diction; Jeff's terms, derived from active verbs, suggest a closer connection to his immediate experience than Adele's abstract nouns convey. Adele can dispose of the bewildering contradictions in her lover's behavior by categorizing her as a "wonderful example of double personality" (QED, 81). Jeff, who does not have this kind of terminology at his disposal, has to work harder to come to terms with the same phenomenon in Melanctha:

> "Melanctha Herbert," began Jeff Campbell, "I certainly after all this time I know you, I certainly do know little, real about you. You see, Melanctha, it's like this way with me[.] . . . You see it's just this way, with me now, Melanctha. Sometimes you seem like one kind of a girl to me, and sometimes you are like a girl that is all different to me, and the two kinds of girls is certainly very different to each other, and I can't see any way they seem to have much to do, to be together in you. They certainly don't seem to be made much like as if they could have anything really to do with each other." (TL, 138)

Jeff's hesitations, his new beginnings, his repetitions, concretely embody the slow revolutions of his mind as he tries to define his contradictory feelings about Melanctha. His distortions of syntax ("much to do, to be together," "much like as if") function as linguistic symptoms of his inability to make a logical connection between the two extremes of Melanctha's personality. Later in the passage, which closely follows the sequence of Adele's speech in *Q.E.D.*, Jeff's language fails him completely. Adele reports her observation of Helen's "infinitely tender patience that entirely overmasters" her (81). Attempting to describe the same aspect of Melanctha's personality, Jeff is so overwhelmed that he completely loses control of his syntax: "and a kindness, that makes one feel like summer, and then a way to know, that makes everything all over, and all that" (TL, 138).

Throughout the central section of "Melanctha," Adele's succinct formulations are translated into a more limited lexicon and greatly expanded to dramatize the process of Jeff's efforts to comprehend Melanctha and his own experiences. Adele's speeches and interior monologues use abstract nouns in well-formed sentences simply to report the conclusions of her thought; they do not enact the confused, uncertain process of thinking. In "Melanctha," deformations of syntax and repetitions of words and syntactical structures radically foreground the materiality of language as an unwieldy medium the characters must work with, and against, in their efforts to resolve complex moral and emotional issues. Like a Cézanne canvas, the assertive surface of this text resists easy comprehension and forces the reader to participate in its rhythmic patterning. In a Cézanne painting, the artfully patterned surface models the process of perceiving physical objects; in "Melanctha," it embodies the slowly revolving thought processes of the characters as they take shape in language.

Jeff's struggle to understand Melanctha and his own awakening passion dramatizes the extent to which his language shapes and confines his thought. Like Adele, he begins with a moral framework that provides simple binary categories for classifying his experience: "living regular" is "good" and "getting excited" is "bad." When Jeff is introduced into the story, the narrator uses the words "good" and "bad" as if they were reliable, univocal labels, in apparent complicity with Jeff's system of moral judgment. Jeff is "good"; his father is "good"; Melanctha is "good now to her mother" (TL, 110). But in the early part of the story, which presents Melanctha's initiation into sexual and emotional maturity as a "wandering after wisdom," the rich polyvalency of the repeated words "wandering" and "wisdom" eludes moral categorization. In sharp contrast, Jeff confronts Melanctha with a rigid set of moral labels. At first he has her safely categorized: "he did not think that she would ever come to any good" (112); he refuses even to acknowledge that she had a "good mind" (116). As he comes to know her somewhat better, he reverses his initial judgment: "Melanctha really was a good woman, and she had a good mind" (131).

Beginning with their first conversation, Melanctha directly challenges Jeff's conventional notions of goodness:

> You certainly are just too scared Dr. Campbell to really feel things way down in you. All you are always wanting Dr. Campbell, is just to talk about being good, and to play with people just to have a good time, and yet always to certainly keep yourself out of trouble. It don't seem to me Dr. Campbell that I admire that way to do things very much. It certainly ain't really to me being very good. (123)

This episode begins the disintegration of the linguistic and conceptual grid through which Jeff has habitually processed his experience, which begins to break down as his passion for Melanctha strains against its rigid structures. Like Adele's in *Q.E.D.*, Jeff's passion plunges him into a moral dilemma. But Jeff's scruples seem much more narrowly moralistic than Adele's, because both the social taboo of lesbianism and the question of Helen's "prostitution" have been eliminated from this story. Brought up to believe that "real, strong, hot love" is the worst form of "getting excited," bad for himself and his people, he is afraid of sexual passion. When he learns of Melanctha's previous sexual experiences, he judges them unequivocally "bad," but the increasing strength of his feelings for her do not allow him to dismiss her so easily (151). He roughly rejects her first direct sexual advances as "ugly" (155). Although he later accepts them, the ambivalence remains: "It was all so mixed up inside him. All he knew was he wanted very badly Melanctha should be there beside him, and he wanted very badly, too, always to throw her from him" (156). The more desperately he attempts to decide who, and what, is "good" and "bad," the more obviously these words fail to provide a stable framework for moral judgments. His attempts to verbalize his feelings poignantly illustrate the insufficiency of the labels he had previously used so confidently to order his experiences.

As he constantly repeats the words "certainly" and "really" in his increasingly desperate efforts to discover what is "certain" and "real" about his experience, these verbal props signal his actual uncertainty and provide a constant ironic counterpoint to his struggles: [13]

> "I *certainly* am *wrong* now, thinking all this way so lovely, and not thinking now any more the old way I always before was always thinking, about what was the *right* way for me, . . . and then I think, perhaps, Melanctha you are really just a *bad* one, . . . and then I always get so *bad* to you, Melanctha, and I can't help it with myself then, never, for I want to be always *right really* in the ways, I have to do them. I *certainly* do very *badly* want to be *right*, Melanctha, the only way I know is *right*

Melanctha *really*, and I don't know any way, Melanctha, to find out *really*, . . . which way *certainly* is the *real right* way . . . and then I *certainly* am awful *good* and sorry, Melanctha, I always give you so much trouble, hurting you with the *bad* ways I am acting. Can't you help me to any way, to make it all straight for me, Melanctha, so I know *right* and *real* what it is I should be acting. . . . I *certainly* do *badly* want to know always, the way I should be acting."

"No, Jeff, dear, . . . [a]ll I can do now, Jeff, is to just keep *certainly* with my believing you are *good* always, Jeff, and though you *certainly* do hurt me *bad*, I always got strong faith in you, Jeff, more in you *certainly*, than you seem to be having in your acting to me, always so *bad*, Jeff."

"You *certainly* are very *good* to me, Melanctha, . . . and me so *bad* to you always, in my acting. Do you love me *good*, and *right*, Melanctha, always?" (159–60; my emphases)

In *Q.E.D.*, Adele describes a similar conflict in terms of an opposition between "passion" and "Calvinistic influence" or "puritan instincts" (103). In the passage above and elsewhere in "Melanctha," intensive repetition of the simpler words "good" and "bad," frequently in combination with "right" and "wrong," dramatize more directly the impasse these characters have talked themselves into. Jeff and Melanctha call themselves and each other "good" and "bad." In this dense verbal interplay, the repeated words dominate the discourse, not only as adjectives but in other syntactical functions as well. "Bad(ly)" appears twice as an intensifying adverb, in connection with the adjectives "good" and "right," both of which are also brought into play as adverbs as the passage progresses. These shifts of grammatical categories augment the reader's sense of the slippery imprecision of these words. As their repetitions echo throughout the passage, these words are gradually emptied of any univocal meaning, while "really" and "certainly" ironically signal the characters' increasing linguistic helplessness and the impossibility of their ever achieving moral certainty through the unwieldy, ambiguous medium of their language.

Jeff's struggles with language are more intense than Melanctha's. Far from sharing his faith in the power of rational thought to clarify emotional experience, she sees it as an impediment that restricts his understanding: "you never can see anything that ain't just so simple, Jeff, with everybody, the way you always think it" (TL, 168). The conflict between her spontaneous, intuitive nature and Jeff's "cold slow way . . . to feel things in him" (174) re-creates the fundamental opposition between Helen and Adele in Q.E.D. Melanctha is a more eloquent and sympathetic character than Helen, however, and her challenge to Jeff's habits of mind is correspondingly more serious. Accused of being incapable of love because she refuses to "remember right," she strongly defends the greater value of "real feeling every moment when its needed":

> "I certainly do call it remembering right Jeff Campbell, to remember right just when it happens to you, so you have a right kind of feeling not to act the way you always been doing to me, and then you go home Jeff Campbell, and you begin with your thinking, and then it certainly is very easy for you to be good and forgiving with it. No, that ain't to me, the way of remembering Jeff Campbell, not as I can see it not to make people always suffer, waiting for you certainly to get to do it. Seems to me like Jeff Campbell, I never could feel so like a man was low and to be scorning of him, like that day in the summer, when you threw me off just because you got one of those fits of your remembering. No, Jeff Campbell, its real feeling every moment when its needed, that certainly does seem to me like real remembering." (181)

In "Melanctha," these contrasting rhythms of personality are more directly related to the question of the relationship between language and emotional experience. Jeff is "slow" because his experience is always mediated by rational reflection in language; his responses are always belated. Melanctha distrusts this form of mediation so strongly that she refuses to take responsibility for words she uttered in the past: "You always wanting to have it all clear out in words always, what everybody is always feeling. I certainly don't see a reason, why I should always be explaining to you what I mean by what I am just saying. . . . I never know anything right I was saying" (171). For her, "it ain't much use to talk about what a woman is really feeling in her" (135). Like Helen in *Q.E.D.*, she sees a fundamental incompatibility between "thinking" and "feeling" (132), but because she is both a more sympathetic and a more articulate character than Helen, her position has a more powerful presence in "Melanctha" than Helen's has in the earlier text.

This opposition between rational analysis and emotional immediacy was one of Stein's central preoccupations during the early years of her career, beginning with her ironic re-creation of her own painful conflict with May Bookstaver in *Q.E.D.* and culminating in *Tender Buttons*. "Melanctha," widely praised for its "colloquial realism," was a crucial step in the process that would lead Stein far beyond the boundaries of conventional realism. Melanctha's articulated opposition to Jeff's habits of mind is only one of the many ways in which this text undermines the supreme value Adele (and, presumably, once Stein herself) invested in rational thought and expression. Time and again, its forceful demonstrations of how coercively the characters' language controls—and impedes—their perceptions and judgments prefigure the radical iconoclasm of *Tender Buttons*.

Jeff learns more from his experience than Adele ever does. Gradually his speeches demonstrate to him, as well as to the reader, how inadequate his language and the conceptual framework it dictates are to the moral and emotional complexity of his experience. Through his verbal struggles with Melanctha and with his own passions, Jeff gradually comes to doubt his own habitual intellectual stance: "Perhaps what I call my thinking ain't really so very understanding" (135). As he abandons his efforts to rationalize his experiences and allows himself simply to feel them, he begins to achieve for himself the "real wisdom" of passionate life that Melanctha already possesses. When he begins to sense the loss of her love, he asks for verbal assurances, but he can no longer be comforted by her repeated declarations that she loves him. Aware now of the gap between language and the reality of emotional experience, he "could not make an answer to Melanctha. What was it he should now say to her? What words could help him to make their feeling any better?" (198). At the end of *Q.E.D.*, Adele reverts to her habits of abstract categorization as a means of distancing and controlling her pain; she dismisses Helen by labeling her a "prostitute" (121, 127). Jeff, with more wisdom, cannot use such words to deny his feelings. Even after he has lost Melanctha, he "always had strong in him the meaning of all the new kind of beauty Melanctha Herbert once had shown him, and always more and more it helped him with his working for himself and for all the colored people" (TL, 207).

Jeff's gradual attainment of this wisdom that transcends moral categories is ironically framed by Melanctha's involvement with Rose Johnson, who represents the unreflective, formulaic morality that initially governed Jeff's habits of thought. The text begins and ends with Melanctha's fatal emotional dependence on Rose, who "had strong the sense of proper conduct" (88). Ignoring Melanctha's years of faithful friendship and service, Rose harshly condemns her dealings with men as unequivocally "bad" and banishes Melanctha from her house with absolute self-righteousness. Rose mindlessly repeats the words "good" and "bad," "right" and "wrong," which were demonstrated to be so problematic in Jeff's struggles to achieve "wisdom." As Melanctha is bludgeoned by these repetitions in a rejection that finally breaks her spirit and leads to her early death, the text offers its final, ironic demonstration of the terrible power of these words both to shape and to impede judgment, by restricting thought to the categories they create.

Repetition is central to the mode of realism Stein created in "Melanctha," a densely patterned textual surface that models the process by which thoughts take shape in language. Although it makes use of some syntactical features common to nonstandard dialects, the language of "Melanctha" is not a literal transcription of Black English but a stylization of the speech and thought patterns of characters whose language is inadequate to their experience. Although the simple words the characters use are shown to be slippery, unstable instruments, their patterning forcefully enacts the play of passions, the frustrating processes of thought and communication. Wordsworth, a century before Stein, discovered the power of repetition to imitate the "craving in the mind" to bridge the gap between intense emotion and inadequate means of expression:

> There is a numerous class of readers who imagine that the same words cannot be repeated without tautology: this is a great error: virtual tautology is much oftener produced by using different words when the meaning is exactly the same. Words, a Poet's words, more particularly, ought to be weighed in the balance of feeling, and not measured by the space which they occupy upon paper. For the Reader cannot be too often reminded that Poetry is passion: it is the history or science of feelings; now every man must know that an attempt is rarely made to communicate impassioned feelings without something of an accompanying consciousness of the inadequateness of our own powers, or the deficiencies of language. During such efforts there will be a craving in the mind, and as long as it is unsatisfied the Speaker will cling to the same words, or words of the same character. There are also various other reasons why repetition and apparent tautology are frequently beauties of the highest kind. Among the chief of these reasons is the interest which the mind attaches to words, not only as symbols of the passion, but as *things*, active and efficient, which are of themselves part of the passion.[14]

Wordsworth's project, like Stein's, was to explore the motions of the human mind in the medium of language. In poems like "The Thorn," the occasion for these reflections, he created personae with limited powers of expression, whose verbal repetitions function mimetically, to dramatize their struggles to formulate their experiences in language. As Wordsworth observed, repetition foregrounds the materiality of language, of words "not only as symbols of the passion, but as *things*, active and efficient, which are of themselves part of the passion." Far more radically than Wordsworth, Stein used repetition in "Melanctha" to undermine the functioning of words as univocal "symbols of the passion" while emphasizing their irreducible power to shape the process of thought.

But for Stein, as for Wordsworth, repetition has other uses as well. Repetition of words, sound, and syntactical patterns plays a major role in structuring poetic language. In "Melanctha," the characters' speeches have their own "beauties" of sound and rhythm, even as they demonstrate the speakers' linguistic inadequacy. Passages of direct narration use the same verbal texture and rhythm to create a rich evocation of simple, elemental patterns of action. In the following passage, repetition reveals not linguistic helplessness but poetic power:

> From the time that Melanctha *was* *tw*elve until she *was* sixteen she *wandered*, al*wa*ys seeking but never more than very dimly seeing *wisdom*. . . .
>
> Melanctha's *wanderings* after *wisdom* she al*wa*ys had to do in secret and by snatches, for her mother *wa*s then still living and 'Mis' Herbert al*wa*ys did some *watching*. . . .
>
> In these days Melanctha talked and stood and *walked* *w*ith many kinds of men. . . . They all supposed her to have *world* knowledge and experience. They, believing that she knew all, told her nothing, and thinking that she *wa*s deciding *w*ith them, asked for nothing, and so though Melanctha *wandered widely*, she *wa*s really very safe *w*ith all the *wandering*.
>
> It *wa*s a very *wonderful* experience this safety of Melanctha. . . . Melanctha herself did not feel the *wonder*. . . .
>
> She knew she *wa*s not getting *w*hat she so badly *wanted*. . . .
>
> Melanctha liked to *wander*, and to stand by the railroad yard, and *watch* the men and the engines and the s*w*itches and everything that *wa*s busy there, *working*. . . . For a child *watching* through a hole in the fence above the yard, it is a *wonder world* of mystery and movement. (TL, 97–98; my emphases)

The lush surface texture flaunts its poetic play of alliteration, rhyme, and repetition of words. The repeated alliteration of *w* and *m*, the major sound motifs of the passage, contrasts with the repetition of sibilants and hard *k* sounds. Participial endings create a network of rhyme. Throughout the passage, sound creates a network of connections independent of syntax, which has a powerful semantic function. As the pattern of words beginning with *w* gradually unfolds, "wandered" and "wisdom" establish the theme and set in motion the associative chain that follows. Wandering, wanting, walking, watching, the men working—forms of these verbs recur, echoing through this passage and the pages that follow. The nouns "wonder," "world," and "wisdom" entwine themselves in this network of sound associations. A second alliterative chain links Melanctha first to her mother and then to the "mystery and movement" of the world of men. At the beginning, Melanctha's mother is watching her; by the end, Melanctha herself is watching the men working. Finally, several pages later, the words "woman" and "wife" appear to complete the sequence (103). As it gradually unfolds in the linear movement of the passage, this interplay of phonemic repetition and difference creates a rhythmic sound pattern that powerfully reinforces the life pattern of emerging sexual awareness that is the theme of the passage.

This long passage is the only section of "Melanctha" that makes systematic use of repetition to embody the rhythm of a life process. This text demonstrates the impotence of repetition, in the speeches and thoughts of its characters, more systematically than its power. In both cases, repetition is used to model the rhythm of a temporal process, and the realism inheres in the material patterning of language, foregrounded to create an iconic figuration of the object it models. After completing *Three Lives*, Stein soon lost interest in the problem of representing the speech and thought patterns of characters whose command of the language is limited and concentrated on exploring the power of repetition to render her own synoptic vision of characters and life processes.

History as Repetition: *The Making of Americans*

A

S early as 1903, Stein had begun writing a novel based on the lives of members of her family.[1] After completing "Melanctha" in 1906, she returned to this project and worked on it for the next five years. The final version of *The Making of Americans* was shaped by her increasingly radical commitment to presenting repetition as the "reality" that informs human history. The 1909 aesthetic credo that begins by invoking the "reality" of Cézanne and Caliban concludes with the declaration, "I believe in repetition. Yes. Always and always, Must write the eternal hymn of repetition" (NB-D, 11). *The Making of Americans* began as a straightforward family chronicle, but it soon became Stein's "eternal hymn of repetition." Its complete title, *The Making of Americans Being a History of a Family's Progress*, seems to align the novel with the optimistic view of history as revelation of human progress that dominated most eighteenth- and nineteenth-century historiography. But its opening paragraph introduces an alternative paradigm that radically challenges this idea of history:

> Once an angry man dragged his father along the ground through his own orchard. "Stop!" cried the groaning old man at last, "Stop! I did not drag my father beyond this tree."
> (MOA, 3)

Repetition, not a linear sequence of discrete events linked in a chain of causality that manifests progress, is the form and force of history in Stein's text.

In 1843 Kierkegaard posited repetition as the "modern life-view," the "new category which has to be brought to light."[2] He was not mistaken. Writers as diverse as Nietzsche, Marx, Spengler, and Yeats explored patterns of repetition in history, while Freud established the repetition compulsion as a motive force in individual lives. Stein's 1908 notebooks reveal that, some years before, her initial confrontation with the idea of history as repetition had shattered her faith in historical progress and, at first, had left her profoundly depressed (NB-14, 7). By the time she began the final draft of *The Making of Americans*, however, she had come to see repetition as a positive force that resolves the apparent chaos of human history and of individual lives into reassuring patterns of orderly recurrence.

In *The Making of Americans*, "repeating in each one makes a history" of individuals and of family life as well (MOA, 192). Characters repeatedly reveal what Stein calls their "bottom natures"; as they repeat themselves, they repeat variations of their parents' essential personality traits. The first chapter presents the Hersland and Dehning families as two closed sets of personality types which, in different "mixtures," pass from parents to children. These characters repeat themselves within a larger field as well, the "simple middle class monotonous tradition, . . . always there and to be always repeated, . . . worthy that all monotonously shall repeat it" (34). In the early draft, these families are German. Shifting the focus away from particularized chronicle to collective history of "[t]he old people in a new world, the new people made out of the old," the final version leaves their country of origin unspecified (3). The Herslands and Dehnings are presented as "ordinary kinds of families" whose "repeating, common, decent enough kind of living" typifies the American middle class (34).

The story Stein's novel tells of the making of these Americans hardly supports the optimism of its title. After coming to America, the children of the immigrants make "substantial progress . . . in wealth, in opportunity, in education" (42). Henry Dehning and the elder David Hersland both become rich. Their children are born with all the material advantages their parents' generation struggled hard to achieve. Early in the novel, Henry Dehning challenges his children, "[T]ell me exactly what you are going to get from all these your expensive modern kinds of ways of doing . . . I say you tell me just what you are going to do, to make it good all this money. Well what, what are all these kinds of improvements going to do for you" (9). After the first chapter, the narrative focuses, in turn, on four members of the children's generation. As in many classic realist novels, business and marriage are the two major spheres of adult activity in *The Making of Americans*. But in Stein's text, circumstantial details are kept to a minimum, to emphasize the monotonous regularity of this middle-class tradition. In these spheres, none of the children's lives presents a striking record of continuing "progress." Martha Hersland's marriage fails; and the marriage of Alfred Hersland and Julia Dehning is not a happy one. Neither Alfred nor David Hersland continues the material success of their father's generation. David achieves a high degree of sensitivity and understanding, but he dies young, without having done much of anything. Even the elder David Hersland, the paragon of middle-class success, loses his fortune before the end of the novel.

The beginning of the novel is situated ambivalently between satire and celebration of this "monotonous middle-class tradition." The account of Julia Dehning's marriage (8–33) satirizes bourgeois American tastes and attitudes "twenty years ago, in the dark age" (28). The narrator proclaims her affection for this tradition, while announcing her geographical and personal separation from it, "here in the heart of a people who despise it" (34). A reworking of the 1903 manuscript, this section is a kind of palimpsestic recapitulation of Stein's early narrative styles. It contains elaborate physical descriptions of characters and settings, the kind of circumstantial details Stein eliminated in the course of writing *Three Lives*, as well as traces of the archly archaic style she affected in the 1903 draft. Characters utter long speeches, in the rhythmically repetitive colloquial style of *Three Lives*, which is the dominant style of the surrounding narrative as well. As the text progresses, however, the characters' voices are soon silenced and the circumstantial details of their lives disappear; all that remains is the omnipresent voice of the author, composing her "hymn of repetition."

Early in the first chapter, the narrator warns the reader that her characters will lack "vital singularity" because America mass-produces its youth in a uniform mold:

> I say vital singularity is as yet an unknown product with us, we
> who in our habits, dress-suit cases, clothes and hats and ways
> of thinking, walking, making money, talking, having simple
> lines in decorating, in ways of reforming, all with a metallic
> clicking like the type-writing which is our only way of think-
> ing, our way of educating, our way of learning, all always the
> same way of doing, all the way down as far as there is any way
> down inside to us. We all are the same all through us, we never
> have it to be free inside us. No brother singulars, it is sad here
> for us, there is no place in an adolescent world for anything ec-
> centric like us, machine making does not turn out queer things
> like us, they can never make a world to let us be free each one
> inside us. (47)

First identifying with this culturally determined uniformity, the
narrator suddenly asserts her own alienated individuality. Halfway
through the first chapter, however, the author begins to develop
a theory of character that will swallow up all individualizing differences, including her own, in a universal typological system:

> There are many kinds of men, of every kind of them there
> are many millions of them many millions always made to be
> like the others of that kind of them, of some kinds of them
> there are more millions made like the others of such a kind of
> them than there are millions made alike of some other kinds of
> men. Perhaps this is not really true about any kind of them,
> perhaps there are not less millions of one kind of men than
> there are millions of other kinds of them, perhaps one thinks
> such a thing about some kinds of men only because in some
> kinds of men there is more in each one of such a kind, more in
> the many millions of such a kind of them, of an individual feel-
> ing in every one of such a kind of them. (115)

Classic realist narratives create the double illusion that their characters are unique individuals and at the same time representa-
tives of social types. When Balzac compares his inventory of social
types in the *Comédie humaine* to the zoological species isolated by

natural historians, he relishes the vast array of social types with their multitude of distinguishing features.³ As the preceding passage suggests, Stein's typological system emphasizes identities and ignores the particularizing differences of social and historical circumstances. Repetition of a limited set of psychological types, first presented in terms of a specific genealogical and cultural heritage, becomes a universal phenomenon.

Stein's notebooks reveal that her reading of Otto Weininger's *Sex and Character* in 1908 was the catalyst for this new project, which led her to transform a chronicle of an American family into a synchronic study of "kinds." Weininger's "science of character" proposed a new "doctrine of the whole" to challenge the empirical psychology of William James. Leaving behind the "motley world, the changing field of sensations," Weininger sought to identify the "permanent existing something" that underlies the "fleeting changes" of psychic life:

> The character, however, is not something seated behind the thoughts and feelings of the individual, but something revealing itself in every thought and feeling. . . . Just as every cell bears within it the characters of the whole individual, so every psychical manifestation of a man involves not merely a few little characteristic traits, but his whole being, of which at one moment one quality, at another moment another quality, comes into prominence.
>
> Just as no sensation is ever isolated, but is set in a complete field of sensation, the world of the Ego, of which now one part and now the other, stands out more plainly, so the whole man is manifest in every moment of the psychical life, although, now one side, now the other, is more visible. This existence, manifest in every moment of the psychical life, is the object of characterology.⁴

Even while Stein was working with William James at Harvard, she was already more interested in her own intuitive perceptions of character than in her teacher's empirical research methods. Her essay "Cultivated Motor Automatism," published in the *Psychologi-*

*cal Review* of May 1898, concerns itself less with the subjects' automatic behavior than with their characters, which she divided into two basic types. She described one type as "nervous" and "intensely interested," the other as "phlegmatic."[5] The schematic opposition first sketched in this essay is more fully elaborated in the contrasting, and conflicting, personalities of the lovers portrayed in *Q.E.D.* and "Melanctha." The last chapter of the 1903 draft of *The Making of Americans* clumsily introduces another version of it: "[p]assionate women, those in whom emotion has the intensity of sensation," are opposed to women who "know not passion" and who "make a resisting compacting mass" to protect themselves (MOA, 169). Julia Dehning, representing the first type, "rushed upon her sorrow, passionately, fervently heroically" (170). Her sister Bertha is presented as her opposite, one of the kind that "sits still" (170). The final version of the novel eliminates this chapter, and this character, but the fundamental opposition it introduced becomes part of the binary system of classification Stein began to construct in 1908.

Although Weininger's book stimulated her to systematize her understanding of character, the typology she created in the novel was purely her own. In her notebooks, she briefly experimented with Weininger's polarities of male and female, the central categories of his binary system: "Picasso has a maleness that belongs to genius. Moi ausi" (NB-C, 21). But his misogynistic treatment of sexual differences did not provide a useful model for Stein's analysis of character. For a time, she also used some of Weininger's categories (prostitute, mother, servant, saint, masculine woman, and lady), plus a few of her own invention (mistress and spinster), to analyze her acquaintances in her notebooks. The categories of servant girl and spinster appear in the first chapter of the novel, illustrated by long "histories" of three governesses and three dressmakers who have worked for the Hersland family.[6] But the two broad categories, "dependent independent" (the "resisting" type) and "independent dependent" (the "attacking" type), clearly derive from the fundamental opposition that governed Stein's presentation of character in her earlier narratives. First introduced to label two contrasting "ways of loving," these soon became the corner-stones of her elaborate system for classifying the "bottom natures" that inform all human behavior (MOA, 165).

Once she had firmly established the foundatons of this system, her desire to illustrate its universal truth came into direct conflict with the exigencies of narrative verisimilitude. "I want sometime to be right about everyone. I want sometime to write a history of everyone, of every kind there is in men and women" (MOA, 574). Constantly subjecting her writing to the demand of "being right," Stein changed her narrative strategies a number of times, as her pursuit of the "reality" she sought to understand and render in language became increasingly incompatible with the conventions governing fictional *vraisemblance*. By the end of the first chapter, the author is chafing at the limits imposed by the fictional world of her story:

> Sometime there will be written a long book that is a real history of every one who ever were or are or will be living from their beginning to their ending, now there is a history of the Hersland and the Dehning families and every one who ever came to know them. (285)

In the second chapter, in complete defiance of novelistic conventions, the author simply abandons her story of the Herslands and Dehnings to write her own "history of getting completed understanding" of human nature, and the project that began as a fictional narrative of three generations of an American family is transformed into a universal, synchronic "history of everyone who ever were or are or will be living" (294).

*The Making of Americans* systematically violates the reader's expectation that the structure of a novel should roughly correspond to the succession of events in the story it narrates. But, beginning in the first chapter, the text inscribes another history in its temporal dimension, the author's quest for "completed understanding." Midway through the first chapter, the construction of the system becomes the dominant action of the text. The Herslands' three governesses and dressmakers are introduced not because they are necessary to the Hersland story but to contribute to a "kind of diagram for a beginning" (225). Their "histories" occupy nearly as much space in the chapter as those of family members, because "[e]very kind of history about any one is important" to the author's study of "kinds" (193). As storytelling is increasingly subordinated to system building, the linearity of writing (and reading) is activated to trace the gradual unfolding of knowledge: "Slowly there is building up a solid structure of the two different kinds of nature" (279).

From the beginning, the reader is invited to identify with the writer of the text more directly than with its fictional characters: "We need only realise our parents, remember our grandparents and know ourselves and our history is complete" (3). The fictional story of the Herslands and Dehnings is subordinated to this collective history, based on personal experience. "Realising" and "remembering" are presented as two essentially different kinds of knowledge; only the first is "present to our feelings" (7, 9). Repeated throughout the text, the word "realise" explicitly aligns Stein's project with Cézanne's reiterated goal of "realizing" his sensations and emphasizes the primary value of direct present-tense experience in this search for knowledge. Narrative, whether historical or fictional, is almost always governed by the past tense; its story has already concluded before the writing, or the reading, begins. Emile Benveniste has sketched the fundamental opposition between *histoire* (pure narration) and *discours* (discourse) in terms of their different systems of time and pronoun reference. Discourse is governed by the first person and the present tense; its other tenses have meaning in relation to the (always present) time of the speaker at the moment of discourse. Pure narration, on the contrary, excludes the first person and the present tense and, with them, all reference to the instance of discourse. "No one speaks. Events seem to tell themselves," within a past-tense system detached from any reference to the situation of discourse.[7] As Benveniste acknowledges, *histoire* rarely exists in this pure state; to a greater or lesser degree, discursive elements penetrate the narration, momentarily breaking its illusory autonomy. From the beginning, *The Making of Americans* freely combines these two systems, often within a single paragraph:

> Henry Dehning was a grown man and for his day a rich
> one when his father died away and left them. Truly he had
> made everything for himself very different; but it is not as
> a young man making himself rich that we are now to feel him,
> he is for us an old grown man telling it all over to his children.
> He is a middle aged man now when he talks about it all to
> his children, middle aged as perhaps sometimes we ourselves
> are now to our talking, but he, he is grown old man to our
> thinking. (7)

As the past tense of the events cedes to the present tense of discourse, the character is moved out of the autonomous time frame of
pure narration into the "now" of the discursive moment. This oscil-
lation of tenses recurs throughout the text, as the discourse constantly breaks the illusionistic closure of the fictional past to make
itself "present to our feeling."

The temporal dimension of the text traces the author's gradual
accumulation of knowledge, which she slowly unfolds for the reader. Direct addresses to the reader soon cease, as she becomes less
confident of her audience. She begins the second chapter with the
admission, "I am writing for myself and strangers. This is the only
way that I can do it" (289). This "I . . . writing" is clearly not a fictional persona. It is the author, stripped of particularizing autobiographical details, seeking knowledge in this process of writing.
The truths she discovers, formulated in the present tense, alternate
with the past tense of narrative: "Mary *was* not a complete one of
such a kind of them. This *is* the kind they are then. Mabel Linker
*was* not at all such a kind of one. This *is now* a description of them"
(231; my emphases). As this passage demonstrates in miniature,
her discourse constantly engulfs the narrative and its individual
characters in the ongoing "now" of her synchronic understanding
of "kinds." Understanding becomes simultaneous with writing: "I
am writing everything as I am learning anything" (540). The discourse, with its ubiquitous formula "as I was saying," constantly
calls attention to itself as an activity unfolding in time. The verbs
"know," "understand," and "think" regularly occur in the present
progressive aspect:

Always more and more I am understanding. (407)

[A]lways then sometime each one I am ever knowing is a whole one to me. (328)

I am thinking just now certainly thinking just now about some men, about some women. (684)

This unusual usage, which transforms these normally stative verbs into verbs of activity, further emphasizes that knowledge, in this text, is not a static state but a temporal process occurring within the ongoing present of the discourse.[8] This path to wisdom, far from smooth, corresponds neither to the linear, chronological order of narrative nor to the logical order of conventional expository prose. Constant false starts and new beginnings, the "irrelating" and "dulling" effects of textual repetition, are all embedded in the discourse. This enormously long book is the antithesis of what Roland Barthes calls a *texte de plaisir*:

> Text of pleasure: which contents, fills, produces euphoria; which comes from culture and does not break with it, is linked to a *comfortable* reading practice. Text of bliss: which imposes a state of loss, which discomforts (perhaps to the point of some boredom), shakes the historical, cultural, psychological assumptions of the reader, the consistency of his tastes, his values, and his memories, brings his relationship to language into crisis.[9]

Resolutely refusing to provide the traditional pleasures of narrative verisimilitude, this text forces its audience to share the author's slow, painful movement toward knowledge in the process of reading.

The second chapter of *The Making of Americans* describes the author's process of understanding, which shapes the entire text:

> Sometimes some one for many years is baffling. The repeated hearing, seeing, feeling of repeating in them does not give to me then a history of the complete being in them. Slowly then sometime it comes to be clearer of them, I begin again with listening, I feel new shades in repeating, parts of repeating

that I was neglecting hearing, seeing, feeling come to have a
louder beating. Slowly it comes to a fuller sounding, sometimes many years pass in such a baffling listening, feeling, seeing all the repeating in some one. Then slowly such a one
comes to have real meaning. Many times I begin and then
begin again. Always I must not begin a deadened following,
always their repeating must be a fresh feeling in my hearing,
seeing, feeling. Always I must admit all changing. Always I
must have a sensitive and open being, always I must have a loving repeating being. Often listening to them is irritating, often
it is dulling, always then there must be in me new beginning,
always there must be in me steadily alive inside me my loving
repeating being. Then sometime every one is a completed being to me, sometime every one has a completed history to me.
Always then it comes out of them their whole repeating, sometime then I can feel and hear and see it all and it has meaning.
Sometime then each one I am ever knowing comes to be to me
a completed being, and then always they are always repeating
always the whole of them. (304–5)

In this section, numerous paragraphs retrace this same pattern,
with only slight variations. Stein's method is circular, constantly returning to her own "loving repeating being" as both origin and
final guarantor of the truth she seeks. As one "having loving repeating as a way to wisdom," repetition is both the object of her study
and its method: "by repeating I come to know it" (299, 293). The
larger structure of the text deliberately models the process sketched
in the preceding paragraph:

[A]lways it has to be told as it has been learned by me very
slowly, each one only slowly can know it, each one must wait
for little pieces of it, always there will be coming more and
more of it, always there will be a telling of every way the two
kinds of being are different in everything and always it is hard
to say it the differences between them, always more and more
I know it, always more and more I know it, always more I
come back to begin again the knowing of it, always I will tell it
as I learned it, sometime I will have told all of it, always I am

telling pieces of it, more and more I will know it, more and more I will tell it, sometime it will be clear to some one and I will be then glad of it. (350)

Stein freely confesses her fears of failure, her increasingly desperate need for an orderly system to unify the disconnected "pieces" of her experience. Her desperate struggle for understanding dominates the entire text. Stein's pursuit of a quixotic dream of total knowledge ends in inevitable failure, but *this* story, which gradually unfolds in the text, makes more compelling reading than the family chronicle it displaces.

Stein's initial premise that character repeatedly reveals itself in individual lives and in family history does not radically differ from the assumptions governing the treatment of character in classic realist narratives. They too present character as a fairly stable entity that manifests itself repeatedly in diverse actions. In family chronicles, character is part of the genealogical heritage that passes from one generation to the next. In traditional novels, however, repetition is subordinated to particularizing differences. Recurrences of personality traits are encoded in a highly particularized linear plot. Family chronicles use inherited similarities of character to highlight the historical circumstances that change the lives of different generations. Patricia Tobin's recent study, *Time and the Novel: The Genealogical Imperative*, focuses on the undermining of "time . . . understood as a linear manifestation of the genealogical destiny of events" in twentieth-century family narratives. Tobin never mentions Stein's *Making of Americans*, but her discussion of the difference between Mann's conventional use of repetition in *Buddenbrooks* and Lawrence's in *The Rainbow* suggests the much greater divergence of Stein's project from traditional family chronicles: "This sameness of experience [in *The Rainbow*] is totally different from Mann's use of the same quality in each generation as the specification of difference, which will allow him to chart decline; rather, sameness here deprives the individual of the unique and singular quality of historical time, and promotes a sense of his or her placement within larger, eternal patterns."[10] The opening pages of Stein's novel use repetition of character traits to trace the rise and decline of her families, but the author quickly became more interested in analyzing, classifying, and describing character as a universal phenomenon than in narrating the particular chain of events or even the larger patterns of action that constitute the experience of a specific family.

Early in the first chapter, the account of Julia Dehning's wedding, adapted from the 1903 draft, uses a conventional device to emphasize the generational recurrence of personality traits. Julia "hit the ground as she walked with the same hard jerking with which her mother Mrs. Dehning always rebuked her husband's sinning" (15). Julia's repetition of this characteristic gesture of her mother, described in almost identical words two pages before, illustrates the extent to which the "stamp" of her mother's nature "went deep, far deeper than just for the fair good-looking exterior" (14). As the author examines the relationship between actions and essential "being" more rigorously, she soon discards this traditional method of using a particular gesture to symbolize a personality trait and focuses, instead, on rendering the larger patterns of action that underlie all the specific activities of a character. The elder David Hersland was "always beginning, beginning was living to him" (120). His "ways of eating, his ways of doctoring, his ways of educating" his children, "his ways of changing," all manifest the same tendency to begin a project enthusiastically and then become impatient and bored (123). This pattern, which pervades all his activities, dominates his chronological history as well:

> David Hersland was such a one when he was *in each of his beginnings, soon then* he would be filled up with impatient feeling *and then* there would be in him less of such a big feeling to every one who then looked at him, *later in his life* he was old and weakening and he *then* was shrunk away from the outside of him, he *then* did not have inside him enough to fill him, he was not *then* a big man to every one who saw him. (121; my emphases)

This one-sentence paragraph begins with a recurring action and shifts to chronological progression, as the largest pattern of his life duplicates that of his every action. Many similarly constructed paragraphs, moving freely from the "now" of the narrative moment to the future "then," repeat the history of David Hersland's future decline (87–88, 92–93). Others trace the same pattern as a generalized history of his "kind." According to the theory of character that is developing in the text, these patterns do not resolve themselves into a meaningful "whole" until old age:

> In the middle of their living they are always repeating, everybody always is repeating in all of their whole living but in the middle of the living of most men and many women it is hard to be sure about them just what it is they are repeating, they are in their living saying many things then and it is hard to know it about them then what it is in them they are repeating that later in their living will show itself to be the whole of them to any one who wants to watch them. (139)

The repeated synopses of David Hersland's life, which collapse a life span into a sentence, demonstrate how radically this text violates the traditional linearity of narrative to enforce its alternative model of the significant form of human life.

Stein's sentences became longer and longer as she attempted "to put the whole history of the human heart on the head of a pin."[11] The phrase is Faulkner's, who described his own characteristic long sentences as an "attempt to get [a character's] past and possibly his future into the instant in which he does something." Stein was less interested in the specific actions her characters perform than in who they are, but her long sentences present their essential "being" as an ongoing process, not as a static state. They systematically transform past-tense verbs of specific action into the progressive aspect or into participial or gerundival constructions and substantive nouns into gerunds. All of these syntactical procedures create a pervasive sense of continuing activity, unbroken by the finality of simple past-tense verbs of action. As Linda McMiniman has observed, Stein's essential being is "'permanent action.' It is knowable because of its recurrence, but it defies accurate depiction in the normal noun-laden language of everyday use."[12] In *Three Lives*, Stein used syntactical deformations to render the colloquial speech styles of her characters and to explore their linguistic limitations. In *The Making of Americans*, however, she systematically deviated from syntactical norms in order to embody in language a new vision of truth.

The more intensively she concentrated on pursuing the truth of "being," however, the more widely her perception of this human essence began to diverge from its original grounding in actions. The more centrally she focused on the problem of identifying, and rendering, this "bottom nature" in herself and in others, the more radically she came to question the assumption that actions are reliable manifestations of character. Any plot, any linear sequence of singular events, is contrary to her fundamental intuition that the essential truth of personality is revealed only in the "repeating" that "steadily tells over and over again the history of the complete being" of her characters (293). In a conventional novel, description works in opposition to narration, because it suspends the temporal movement of the story. By the second chapter of Stein's text, a "complete history" becomes synonymous with a "complete description" of essential "being," and repetition of identities supplants diachronic difference as the form of history in *The Making of Americans*.

In this chapter, the author's analysis of her own history leads her to conclude that her own "bottom nature" did not manifest itself in "ordinary living" for many years:

> There was then always in me as a bottom nature to me an earthy, resisting slow understanding, loving repeating being. As I was saying this has nothing to do with ordinary learning, in a way with ordinary living. . . .
>
> As I was saying learning, thinking, living in the beginning of being men and women often has in it very little of real being. Real being, the bottom nature, often does not then in the beginning do very loud repeating. Learning, thinking, talking, living, often then is not of the real bottom being. Some are this way all their living. . . .

> There was a time when I was questioning, always asking, when I was talking, wondering, there was a time when I was feeling, thinking, and all the time then I did not know repeating. There was a long time then when there was nothing in me using the bottom loving repeating being that now leads me to knowing. (301–2)

The first chapter presents larger patterns of action that emerge from the activities of "ordinary living," but as the text progresses, the notion of essential "being" becomes increasingly dissociated from specific actions and these repeated patterns of behavior as well. Already in the first chapter, the author is convinced that children's repeated patterns of action do not reveal their essential natures: "In children as it always is with young living there is much repeating but it is not then so surely themselves they are expressing. . . . [I]n the regular repeating in mostly all children there is less that is really from them more that is just part of the regular living around them" (128). By the time she resumes the narrative of the Hersland family, focusing on the childhood of Martha, she has come to believe so strongly that actions do not reveal character that all narration has become misrepresentation. The anecdote of Martha throwing her umbrella in the mud is narrated twice; both times it is followed by a disclaimer: "it is very hard telling from any incident in any one's living what kind of being they have in them" (388); "this is a description of an action that many very different kinds of children could have been doing when they were left behind struggling" (394). It "does not now help very much" to understand Martha Hersland's character. Even the narrative fact that "[w]hen she was a very little one sometimes she wanted not to be existing" doesn't help to delineate her individual nature, because "[t]his is a very common thing in mostly every one in the beginning" (399). By this time the author has concluded that none of the traditional resources of narrative will serve to reveal her character's "being":

> [I]t is hard to know the kind of being in any one from just a description of some thoughts, some feelings, some actions in

them for it is in their feeling of themselves inside them that the kind of being in them shows in them and that comes out of them slowly in their living, that comes out of them always as repeating, this is very very difficult to make any one understand from a description of them. (399)

In the following chapter, she confesses her inability to imagine connections between actions and "being":

I have not any dramatic imagination for action in them, I only can know about action in them from knowing action they have been doing any of them . . . I cannot ever construct action for them to be doing, I have certainly constructive imagination for being in them. (538)

Stein's insertion of her 1903 narrative *Fernhurst* into chapter 2, with Martha Hersland in the role of the rejected wife, clearly, if unintentionally, illustrates her point. The clumsy reworking of the story does not conceal the lack of connection between descriptions of Martha's "being" and her role in this conventional narrative. The author freely admits "a little shame" at resorting to this expedient of "copying an old piece of writing" that uses "words that sometime had real meaning . . . and have not any real meaning in them to the feeling and the thinking and the imagining" (441). By this point in the text, no words have "real meaning" for her except the limited set of adjectives she has invented to label essential "being."

By the third chapter of the novel, which is entitled "Alfred Hersland and Julia Dehning," Stein's search for "completed understanding" had led her far afield from the family narrative she was still committed to writing. Beginning in the second chapter, the author's own "history" breaks the closure of the Herslands' and Dehnings' fictional world and introduces a vast number of characters unconnected to their story to illustrate the truth of her system. Unnamed, these characters are each referred to only as "this one." The only referent the text occasionally provides for the adjective "this" is interior to the discourse ("this one that I am now beginning describing" [525]). Without specific referents, these adjectives function as deictics, situating these characters in direct relation to the writer in the instance of discourse. Concealing their specific identities, the author teasingly reminds the reader of their objective reality in the world of her immediate experience: "I have told this one that I will tell it then. This one will not know then it is this one. That is the very nice thing in this writing. Sometime I will tell everything, everything. Mostly I do tell anything" (567). Occasionally deictic time references situate the anonymous characters in immediate relation to the time of writing: "I saw yesterday afternoon two of them together" (571); "There were to-night eight of them" (679). For Stein, the proliferation of case histories adds more "reality" to her enterprise:

> Always there are many many millions of every kind of men and women and this makes many stories very much realler, there being so many always of the same kind of them. It makes it realler then when in a story there are twelve women, all alike, and one hundred men, all alike, and a man and a woman completely resembling the one to the other one of them. (395)

By the time she began the task of rendering Alfred Hersland in the third chapter of the novel, Stein's search for understanding had become dizzyingly circular. The text constantly accumulates more "histories" to develop a knowledge of "kinds," but as resemblances become more "real" than differences, each "history" simply repeats the characteristics of the "kind." By the third chapter, these paradigms, which obliterate all traces of individuality, have become the sole means of rendering characters:

> Alfred Hersland then was a kind of them he had a kind of being in him that was in him as more or less engulfing, somewhat passionate, not very bad, certainly not very good, engulfing resisting dependent independent being, needing to own those he would need for loving, very often needing some one poignantly alive to influence him.
> Of the kind of one that Alfred Hersland was in his being

> they range from very good ones through to pretty bad ones,
> from very tyrannical ones to very just ones, from very good
> ones through to pretty bad ones, from very religious ones to
> completely sceptical ones, from very dominant ones to very
> meek ones, from very passionate ones to completely indiffer-
> ent ones and all of these in their living are of the resisting kind
> of them the dependent independent kind of them, those of
> them should have then needing to own those they need for
> loving. (523)

This passage, one of many similar efforts to "realize" Alfred Hersland, demonstrates how tautological Stein's process of rendering
character has become.

When she introduced her major categories into the novel, she
was aware that it would be difficult to communicate her understanding of character in these terms:

> It is true then that always every one is of one kind or the other
> kind of them the independent dependent or the dependent
> independent kind of them. It is hard to tell it about them, to de-
> scribe it how each one is of the kind of them that is in that one.
> *It is hard to tell it about them because the same words can de-
> scribe all of them the one and the other kind of them.* . . . It is
> hard to describe it in them the kind of being each one has in
> them, it is hard to describe it in them it is hard to know it in
> them, it is only slowly the two kinds of them come to be clear
> to every one who listens to the repeating that comes out of
> them, who sees the repeating that is in them the repeating of
> the bottom nature of them. (178; my emphasis)

"Independent dependent" and "dependent independent," each
self-canceling in terms of ordinary lexical meaning, each the mirror
image of the other, are virtually empty signifiers. Their meaning is
more specifically determined inside the text, partly by their systematic association with other pairs of words, such as "attacking"
and "resisting," and partly by the cumulative effect of specific "histories" which are introduced to illustrate the two kinds. But in the

Alfred Hersland chapter, Stein's means of rendering individual "histories" are restricted to the same limited set of words that label essential "being":

> There are only a few words and with these mostly always I am writing that have for me completely entirely existing being, in talking I use many more of them of words I am not living but talking is another thing, in talking one can be saying mostly anything, often then I am using many words I never could be using in writing. In writing a word must be for me really an existing thing, it has a place for me as living, this is the way I feel about me writing. (540)

Moving back and forth from individuals to "kinds," her descriptions endlessly repeat the few words that "have for [her] completely entirely existing being." This circular process, reenacted within an increasingly self-enclosed, self-referential system, demonstrates the impasse toward which Stein's singleminded pursuit of identities had been leading, with its own inexorable logic.

While Stein was working on the previous chapter of the novel, she was analyzing various painters' relationships to their objects in her notebooks. In these analyses she consistently identifies her own work with Cézanne's and Picasso's "direct relationship to the object," their "realisation of the object itself."[13] Throughout *The Making of Americans* her reiterated desire to "realise" her characters explicitly aligns her project with theirs. She repeatedly insists that her knowledge of others is grounded in her immediate experience of them: "They are whole beings then, they are themselves inside them to me. They are then, each one, a whole one inside me. . . . I know it, I am full up with it and I tell it. . . . Sometimes because I am so full of it it keeps pouring out of me all the time when I am first having it" (324, 325, 326). Time and again these metaphors of ingestion and expulsion evoke her intense, even visceral relationship to the objects of her writing.

Stein's perception of Picasso, in her notebooks, as the direct successor to Cézanne's aesthetic goal of creating a "direct relationship to the object" is fundamentally correct. By 1909, however, Picasso's painting had departed radically from Cézanne's lifelong dedication to "realizing" his immediate visual sensations. And the methods of "realizing" her objects that Stein developed as *The Making of Americans* progressed were more closely related to Picasso's recent work than to Cézanne's.

The genesis of Picasso's landmark painting *Les Demoiselles d'Avignon* (1907) indicates the direction of his art during the time Stein was writing her long novel. In an early study, a sailor is seated in the center, surrounded by food, flowers, and five nude women; at the left, a man enters this gay brothel scene carrying a skull.[14] In the final version, nearly all traces of this original anecdotal context have disappeared and, with them, the overt literary symbolism of the early conception. The final version reduces the human anatomy to geometrical outlines and the faces to grotesque, masklike forms. Cézanne's *Baigneuses* provided the most immediate model for this kind of painting, but its style evokes Iberian and African sculpture more directly than Cézanne's compositional techniques.[15] In 1908 Picasso began to use Cézannesque techniques of *passage* and geometrical reduction of objects to create structures of interlocking pictorial planes in the rue des Bois landscapes. In the masterful *Three Women* of the same year, closely fused triangular planes create a pattern of interlocking, low-relief pyramidal forms that covers the entire canvas, uniting human bodies and background in its all-pervasive design. The 1909 *Vase, Gourd, and Fruit on a Table* repeats the same triangular shape in the folds of the tablecloth and napkins, the three figs, and the outline of the tabletop. In the summer of 1909, working in Horta de San Juan, Picasso produced the remarkable series of female heads and the three landscapes that Stein, seconded by many art historians, regarded as the beginning of cubism. The series of female portraits shows an increasingly radical use of interlocking geometrical planes to model human subjects. Geometrical forms pervade the three landscapes as well; some are outlined and shaded to model three-dimensional objects, but most are fused to one another by Cézannesque *passage* to defy resolution into traditional depth perspective. Stein, who had seen Picasso's photographs of the motifs he painted, observed that these three landscapes were "extraordinarily realistic and all the same the beginning of Cubism" (P, 8). While the rectilinear planes that model buidings are derived from the shapes of houses the photograph records, these geometrical shapes are used as a formal motif that imposes its unifying pattern on the entire canvas.

Cézanne's canvases are pervaded by an all-over patterning of colored brushstrokes that notate the painter's sensations of color. Picasso's cubist canvases are dominated by these geometrical planes, fused by a closely hatched *facture* derived from Cézanne's. Although Cézanne's paintings contain innumerable examples of buildings modeled as simple geometric shapes, these rectangular forms never pattern the entire canvas, as they do in Picasso's paintings of this period. The reinterpretation of Cézanne that began after his death in 1907 exalted his dictum, "Everything in nature is modeled on the sphere, the cone, and the cylinder," above his insistence on the primacy of immediate sensation.[16] Cézanne said this to Emile Bernard as a piece of practical, thoroughly conventional advice based on the conventions of perspective painting, but Bernard took it out of context and misinterpreted it as the master's declaration that geometrical forms "are contained in everything we see, they are its invisible scaffolding."[17] Unlike Cézanne, Picasso used geometrical forms as the highly visible scaffolding that structures all his cubist canvases—still lifes, landscapes, and portraits.

During the years Stein was working on *The Making of Americans*, she was intimately acquainted with every new development in Picasso's work. Even when he was away from Paris, he sent her photographs of his most recent paintings.[18] During the summer of 1909, Stein received photographs of the landscapes and portraits that marked the beginning of cubism. Although they corresponded regularly, Picasso, unlike Cézanne, never wrote about the ideas that governed his work. But Leo Stein's memoirs offer a rare glimpse of Picasso expounding the theoretical premises of his cubist period. As Leo's sarcastic tone indicates, he never shared his sister's enthusiasm for Picasso's new mode of realism:

A revolutionary moment succeeded. Picasso began to have ideas. . . . Picasso began to have opinions on what was and what was not real, though as he understood nothing of these matters the opinions were childishly silly. He would stand before a Cézanne or a Renoir picture and say contemptuously, "Is that a nose? No, this is a nose," and then he would draw a pyramidal diagram. "Is this a glass," he would say, drawing a perspective view of a glass. "No, this is a glass," and he would draw a diagram with two circles connected by crossed lines. I would explain to him that what Plato and other philosophers meant by "real things" were not diagrams, that diagrams were abstract simplifications and not a whit more real than things with all their complexities, that Platonic ideas were worlds away from abstractions, and couldn't be pictured, but he was bent now on doing something important—reality was important whatever else it might be, and so Picasso was off.[19]

"Childishly silly" or not, this redefinition of what was "real" apparently stimulated the paintings that revolutionized the Western tradition of representational art. Leo Stein's anecdote suggests that Picasso's ideas as well as the example of his paintings may have stimulated and certainly lent support to the increasingly reductive notion of "reality" Stein was developing as she was writing *The Making of Americans*.

Picasso's diagrammatic, geometrical rendering of his objects parallels Stein's efforts to represent nothing but essential "being" in terms of an all-encompassing system of classification. In her notebooks and in the novel as well, Stein describes both her analysis of individuals and her construction of her system as making "diagrams."[20] John Berger proposes the diagram as the "metaphorical model" of cubism, in terms that are equally applicable to Picasso's project and to Stein's:

> The metaphorical model of Cubism is the *diagram*: the diagram being a visible, symbolic representation of invisible processes, forces, structures. A diagram need not eschew certain aspects of appearances: but these too will be treated symbolically as *signs*, not as imitations or re-creations.
>
> The model of the *diagram* differs from that of the *mirror*

in that it suggests a concern with what is not self-evident. . . . It differs from the model of the *personal account* in that it aims at a general truth.[21]

But C. S. Peirce's more rigorous consideration of the geometrical diagram clarifies the crucial difference between Picasso's diagrammatic reduction of his objects and Stein's. As Peirce emphasizes, the geometrical diagram is an iconic design, a "representamen of what it represents . . . by virtue of its being an immediate image."[22] The pyramidal diagram that Picasso proposes as a "real" nose, however reductive, still has a degree of relational similarity to the object it signifies. Stein's medium is language. She insists that the few words she uses have "completely weight and form and really existing being" for her, but these adjectival labels are still arbitrary signs, which cannot create the "direct relationship to the object" that a geometrical diagram can (MOA, 540).

Years later, Stein came close to admitting that her system of classification failed to provide her with adequate means of "realizing" her objects. In "The Gradual Making of *The Making of Americans*," she acknowledged that her knowledge of "types of people" still left her with the difficulty of "put[ting] into words . . . a whole human being felt at one and the same time" (LIA, 145). To demonstrate that she "became very consciously obsessed by this very definite problem," she went on to quote an anecdote from the Alfred Hersland chapter that concerns a little boy "killing things to make collections" of butterflies and beetles.[23] In its original context, it is not presented as an explicit comment on the author's own project, but, as the later essay suggests, it is an apt comment on the perils of classification. Throughout the novel, Stein insists that she is "full" of her character's essential "being." She declares that the understanding she achieves through her love of repetition is an "earth feeling," identical to the "earthy . . . sense of the significance of objects" that she attributes to Picasso in her notebooks (MOA, 295; NB-A, 19; B, 1). She repeatedly assures the reader that her knowledge of "being" comes from "many years of listening, seeing, living, feeling, loving the repeating" that gradually clarifies individuals' "living, loving, eating, pleasing, smoking, thinking, scolding, drinking, working, dancing, walking, talking, laughing, sleeping" into "completed understanding" (MOA, 307, 290). But her discourse endlessly repeats only the few words that label the conclusions of these observations as she goes on incorporating more and more cases into her paradigms.

The structure of Stein's prose, with its endless repetitions and reformulations, effectively enacts the movements of her own mind, endlessly revolving inside the increasingly restrictive boundaries of her self-created system, but it does not render the process by which she gradually achieved her knowledge of individuals. While her prose repeatedly proclaims her ecstatic union with her objects, the reader, who has no means of sharing in the process, is likely to become bored with these reiterated reports of her conclusions. In *Le Plaisir du texte* (p. 43), Barthes has observed, "Boredom is not far from bliss [*jouissance*]: it is bliss seen from the shores of pleasure." Later in this text (pp. 67–68), Barthes acknowledges that repetition can create this state of bliss: "There are abundant ethnographic examples: obsessive rhythms, incantatory music, litanies, rites, and Buddhist nembutsu, etc.: to repeat excessively is to enter into loss, into the zero of the signified. However: for repetition to be erotic, it must be formal, literal, and in our culture, this flamboyant (excessive) repetition reverts to the eccentric." Many readers have experienced Stein's endless repetitions as this kind of liberation from meaning, although not all have found the experience equally blissful. But Stein never intended this effect; she wanted repetition to render the "last touch of being" of her objects (MOA, 181).

According to Kierkegaard, "When the Greeks said that all knowledge is recollection they affirmed that all that is has been; when one says that life is a repetition one affirms that existence which has been now becomes."[24] Stein describes her experience of repetition in individuals similarly, as a perception that is constantly renewed in the present. But her system of classification works against her desire to "realize" this experience for the reader. As she frequently acknowledges, the search for resemblances is grounded in recollection; classification of "being" presupposed "*completed* understanding" (MOA, 290, 322, 338). Gilles Deleuze begins his study *Différence et répétition* by emphasizing,

"Repetition is not generalization. . . . To repeat is to conduct one-self with regard to something unique or singular, which has no likeness or equivalent." In opposition to this vital singularity, he argues, "Generalization is of the order of laws. But the law deter-mines only the resemblance of subjects who are subjugated to it, and their equivalence to the terms that it designates."[25] In these terms, Stein's two goals were fundamentally incompatible from the beginning; the "law" of her totalizing system inevitably obliterated the essential singularity of her perception of repetition in individual lives. Once this system begins to dominate the text, the figure of repetition itself is the only trace that remains of the experience she intended to "realise."

Many of the most compelling passages in *The Making of Americans* reveal the intensity of Stein's need to perceive individu-als as "whole" and to create an ordered system of resemblances that would reduce the plethora of individual differences to a unified field of knowledge. Early in the novel, she expresses her faith that repetition "gives to every one who feels it in them a more certain feeling about them, a more secure feeling in living. . . . Always more and more then there is contentment in the secure feeling re-peating in every one gives to every one" (227). She soon needs more than this perception of repetition to satisfy her desire for order: "The important thing then [in] hearing, feeling, seeing all the re-peating coming out from such a one is to realise the *meaning* of the being, it is not enough to realise all the repeating in such a one" (318; my emphasis). Her goal is to achieve the "completed friend-ly feeling of the whole being," but in the second chapter the author begins to acknowledge that sometimes she perceives nothing but "pieces" (310, 311). As the text progresses, this sense of frag-mentation increasingly threatens to destroy the validity of the sys-tem. Without the certainty that each individual is a "whole one, a complete one so that there can then be a solid basis of com-parison, . . . there are so many ways of seeing, feeling resemblances in some one, some one resembles so many men and women that it is confusing, baffling, then the one learning kinds in men and women is despairing, nothing then to that one has any meaning, it is then to that one all of it only an arbitrary choosing" (341).

This idea of character as a collection of disconnected pieces was already present in Stein's earlier texts. Adele in *Q.E.D.* and Jeff in "Melanctha" both struggle to comprehend the multiplicity of their lovers' personalities. Significantly, Jeff experiences a sense of unity only after he abandons the conceptual grid of his moral categories and gives in to his feelings: "I got a new feeling now . . . and I see perhaps what really loving is like, like really having everything together, new things, *little pieces all different*, like I always before been thinking was bad to be having, all go together like, to make one good big feeling" (TL, 158; my emphasis). After Stein brilliantly demonstrated the inadequacy of Jeff's attempts to categorize the complexity of Melanctha's personality in the language he has at his disposal, in *The Making of Americans* she tried to forge a language of classification, with an even more limited lexicon than Jeff's, that would master the rich diversity of personality. The author's own language eventually proved to be no more powerful than that of the character she created in "Melanctha." By the Alfred Hersland chapter, if not before, Stein's repetitions seem to demonstrate as much helplessness and futility as Jeff's. The complexity of her own experiences exceeds the restrictions imposed by her conceptual system: "[E]very one is to me just now as pieces to me" (MOA, 520). In this chapter, her persistent inability to "realise" Alfred Hersland makes her doubt her ability to perceive or create the wholeness she so fervently desires. Her increasing sense of fragmentation, which undermines her faith in her totalizing system, produces an outburst of metaphysical despair:

> Why should anything any one keep on going if not ever at any time anything any one will be a whole one . . . now mostly every one is a piece of a one, not all the being as a complete one and yet every one has their own being in them and putting all of each kind of them together to make a whole one can not be to me a satisfaction, cannot give to me any real satisfaction can not be a satisfactory way in my feeling of having completion of having anything or any one a whole one cannot give to me any

reason why the world should keep on being, there is not any reason if in repeating nothing is giving to me a sensation of a completed one. (521)

Within two years, she would embrace this sense of fragmentation as the only "reality" and create a new mode of writing to celebrate it. In 1938 she proclaimed it the "splendor" of the twentieth century:

> The twentieth century is more splendid than the nineteenth century, certainly it is much more splendid. The twentieth century has much less reasonableness in its existence than the nineteenth century but reasonableness does not make for splendor. . . . So the twentieth century is that, it is a time when everything cracks, where everything is destroyed, everything isolates itself, it is a more splendid thing than a period where everything follows itself. So then the twentieth century is a splendid period, not a reasonable one in the scientific sense, but splendid. (P, 48–49)

None of her later writings acknowledges either the agonizing personal struggle that preceded this affirmation or the radical epistemological break between *The Making of Americans* and her later writings. Her totalizing system of classification, however eccentric, was meant to be "reasonable . . . in the scientific sense," resembling the classical taxonomies of natural history. Like Linnaeus's system, Stein's selects one element as a basis for studying identities and differences, ignoring all the rest, and uses it as the determinant of character.[26] Basing her taxonomy on the Jamesian method of introspection supplemented by observation of others' behavior, she analyzed herself and a large number of acquaintances. She was pursuing the ideal order of classical science, a conceptual grid that would impose coherence on the vast field of human behavior.

In the Alfred Hersland chapter, the author's persistent failure to "realise" the central character as a coherent whole creates an increasingly urgent need for total knowledge and increasingly impossible criteria for achieving it. No longer content with paradigms based on identities, she begins to require a different form of comprehensiveness as well. However closely she studies a person, she feels that her observations are always incomplete, because they cannot include "what they are saying to other ones, what they are feeling" (MOA, 610). Eventually her desire for comprehensive factual data becomes so urgent that nothing will satisfy her but a "complete record of each one, what each one did, what each one had as being in her in him, what each one could be doing, thinking, feeling, knowing" (672). Although she has little hope of achieving this knowledge, still she pursues her impossible dream. Exhaustive enumeration becomes her new criterion for mastering the truth: "It would be a very complete thing in my feeling to be having complete lists of every body ever living and to be realising each one and to be making diagrams of them and lists of them and explaining the being in each one and the relation of that being to other beings in other men and other women and to go on then explaining and realising and knowing the complete being in each one and all the kinds there are in men and women" (594–95). In the first chapter of the novel, case histories serve to develop her paradigms, to "make a kind of diagram" of essential being (225). By this point in the text, the paradigm, no longer satisfying in itself, must be supplemented by a complete inventory of every individual. In addition to spawning the innumerable case histories that fill the second and third chapters of the novel, this impulse to produce a comprehensive inventory overflowed into *A Long Gay Book* and *Many Many Women*, both of which began as collections of short descriptions of anonymous individuals.[27] In the Alfred Hersland chapter of the novel, new categories and lists proliferate, as the author frantically pursues her two conflicting ideas of comprehensive knowledge, the totalizing paradigm and the exhaustive inventory.

   The more strongly her continuing empirical observations threaten the unifying coherence of her system, the more clearly her struggles reveal the metaphysical assumptions that impel her quest for totalizing knowledge:

> Sometime I want to be completely certain. I am one that in this way am wanting to be completely certain, am wanting to be right in being completely certain and in this way only in me can

it come to be in me that to be dead is not to be a dead one.
Really to be just dead is to be to me a really dead one. To be
completely right, completely certain is to be in me universal in
my feeling, to be like the earth complete and fructifying. (MOA,
574)

Only a mastery of truth will overcome her terror of meaningless
mortality. For Stein, infancy is the mirror image of death, a discontinuity of consciousness at the time of origin that equally threatens the "universal" feeling:

> There are some when they feel it inside them that it has
> been with them that there was once so very little of them, that
> they were a baby, helpless and no conscious feeling in them,
> that they knew nothing then when they were kissed and dan-
> dled and fixed by others who knew them when they could
> know nothing inside them or around them, some get from all
> this that once surely happened to them to that which was then
> every bit that was then them, there are some when they feel it
> later inside them that they were such once and that was all that
> there was then of them, there are some who have from such
> a knowing an uncertain curious kind of feeling in them that
> their having been so little once and knowing nothing makes it
> all a broken world for them that they have inside them, kills for
> them the everlasting feeling; and they spend their life in many
> ways, and always they are trying to make for themselves a new
> everlasting feeling. (LGB, 13)

Stein's celebration of repetition is an attempt to repair this breach,
but time and again her text obsessively returns to the fact of death,
repeating its haunting refrain, "Dead is dead."[28] Repetition alone
did not suffice to overcome her fear of mortality. Only the certainty
of complete knowledge could give her the "everlasting feeling" she
craved:

> I know then there can be a history of each one and of all kinds
> all the kinds in men and women. This is a pleasant feeling, this
> is comforting to me just now when I am thinking of every one
> always growing older and then dying. . . . [A]s I am saying

I am having a pleasant completely completed feeling and always then it is a comfortable and calming thing this being certain that each one is one of a kind of them in men and women and that there are always very many of each kind existing, that each one has their own being in them is then completely interesting, that each one sometime is to be a dead one is then not discouraging, and so then I am having a completely pleasant and completed feeling, I who am completely certain that each one is of a kind in men and women, I who am always almost always knowing several of each kind of them I come to know in living, I who am expecting sometime perhaps to be knowing all there ever can be, were or are or will be of kinds in men and women. I have then even with sombre certain feeling that each one is always an older one and sometime a dead one I have then knowing each one is of one kind in men and women I have then a pleasant feeling, a contented a completed feeling as I have been saying. I have a quiet sombre feeling I have not so much an afraid feeling in being living now when I am certain, and I am knowing them, that there are a number of kinds in men and women, not such a great number of them, quite a number of them. (MOA, 581)

The author's sense of having achieved this synchronic understanding that obliterates history, by "knowing all there ever can be, were or are or will be of kinds in men and women," is intermittent at best, and it does not help her to resolve the problem of rendering the individual character of Alfred Hersland. In 1910, during this period of struggle recorded in the Alfred Hersland chapter of the novel, she began writing portraits of her friends.[29] Leaving behind the apparatus of her descriptive system, she created a new method of rendering individual personalities in terms of their characterizing actions. At the same time she was mastering this new technique, she was still pursuing the lure of "completed understanding" in the novel. But at the end of the Alfred Hersland chapter, the author announces, "This is the ending of just this way of going on telling about being being in some men and in some women" (719). This proclamation marks the end of Stein's quest for a totalizing system, which had seemed to her the only way of overmastering discontinuity and death. The final chapter of the novel is a powerful rendition of the life and death of David Hersland, written in the style of the early portraits. At the beginning of it, admitting that her quest for complete knowledge is doomed, the author still associates this failure with death:

> I am now again and again certain that I will not ever be realising experiencing in each one of very many men and very many women, I can realise something of experiencing in some of them, in them as kinds of them but I am needing to have it in me as a complete thing of each one ever living and I I know I will not, and I am one knowing being a dead one and not being a living one, I who am not believing that I will be realising each one's experiencing. (729)

David Hersland dies young; his death pervades her somber presentation of his life. After finishing this paean to death, Stein went on to liberate herself and her writing from the certainties of all totalizing systems of knowledge and to celebrate the difference and discontinuity that had seemed so threatening as the "reality" of the twentieth century.

Portraits of Artists and Others

STEIN wrote "Ada," which she always claimed was her first portrait, as a tribute to Alice B. Toklas, who had recently begun living with her (ABT, 114). This apparently spontaneous gesture of affection inaugurated a new mode of rendering character, independent of the descriptive apparatus that absorbed individuals into "kinds" in the novel. Portions of the manuscript of "Ada," including nearly half of the final paragraph, are in Alice B. Toklas's handwriting; perhaps Toklas collaborated in writing her own portrait, as Richard Bridgman has suggested.[1] However it was created, this portrait, especially in its final paragraph, illustrates the new method that proved to be Stein's way out of the impasse she had reached in the Alfred Hersland chapter of *The Making of Americans*. She composed "Ada" in December 1910. By February 1911, she had already written so many portraits that she was planning to publish a short volume of them.[2]

"Ada" begins as a narrative. After briefly recounting the loves of Ada's brother, it tells the story of Ada's family life—her mother's death, her relatives' invasion of her home, their deaths—and her decision to leave home. Embedded in this linear narrative is the repeated motif of "telling" and "listening" to stories, which recurs, in different contexts, in eight sentences of the two paragraphs of Ada's story. The final paragraph celebrates her new life with her lover. Abandoning chronological sequence in favor of continuing actions, it repeats variations of the earlier motif, "telling" and "listening," combined with the new ones, "living" and "loving":

> She came to be happier than anybody else who was living then. It is easy to believe this thing. She was telling some one, who was loving every story that was charming. Some one who was living was almost always listening. Some one who was

loving was almost always listening. That one who was loving
was almost always listening. That one who was loving was
telling about being one then listening. That one being loving
was then telling stories having a beginning and a middle and an
ending. That one was then one always completely listening.
Ada was then one and all her living then one completely telling
stories that were charming, completely listening to stories having a beginning and a middle and an ending. Trembling was all
living, living was all loving, some one was then the other one.
Certainly this one was loving this Ada then. And certainly Ada
all her living then was happier in living than any one else who
ever could, who was, who is, who ever will be living. (GP, 16)

In *The Making of Americans*, Stein had quickly abandoned the idea
of "telling stories having a beginning and a middle and an ending."
In this portrait as well, linear narrative disappears even as it is
being thematized in the final paragraph. Perfective verb forms, used
to narrate a sequence of completed actions in the preceding paragraphs, cede to progressive forms. Dense repetition of words, syntactical patterns, and phonemes (*l* and *w*) create a rhythmical,
melodic surface texture. Sound patterning reinforces the multiple
semantic combinations of the repeated motifs. The prose gradually
forges a web of association that unites Ada and her lover, who
share in these continuing actions, even before their union is explicitly declared: "Trembling was all living, living was all loving,
some one was then the other one." There is no closure in this "happy ending" of Ada's story; all its actions are continuing processes.

The portrait Stein liked to think of as the first one affirms
Ada's uniqueness in words that ironically echo *The Making of
Americans*' goal of creating a "real history of every one who ever
were or are or will be living": Ada is "happier in living than any one
else who ever could, who was, who is, who ever will be living"
(MOA, 285; GP, 16). In the novel, Stein's understanding of character
was informed by a double vision of her objects: "Everybody is
a real one to me, everybody is like some one else too to me, everyone
is a kind of men and women to me" (MOA, 333). But her method
obliterated individual differences in its pursuit of universal resem-

blances. The portraits shift the focus from "kinds" to individuals, characterized by their patterns of habitual actions. "Each one is one" is the jubilant refrain that connects the separate portraits in *Many Many Women* and celebrates the individuality within a crowd in "Galeries Lafayettes": "One, one, one, one, there are many of them. . . . Each one is one, there are many of them. . . . Each one in being one is one being one being especially that one, especially being that one" (PP, 169, 171). All the individuals portrayed in *Many Many Women* are unnamed; each is simply "one." Although the titles of many portraits are generic ("A Man," "Five or Six Men") and others, like "Ada," use fictional proper names, manuscript notes indicate that Stein generally had a particular subject in mind. Even when portraits designate their subjects in their titles, the texts generally use the pronoun "one" throughout. Still, each "one" in the portraits signifies a singular individual, unlike the collective "one" of indefinite reference or the "one of a kind" in *The Making of Americans.*

Even after she began working with this form, Stein did not entirely abandon her interest in resemblances. One series of early portraits, most of which she did not choose to include in her collections *Geography and Plays* (1922) and *Portraits and Prayers* (1934), was clearly an extension of her continuing efforts to systematize her understanding of character in the novel. The Alfred Hersland chapter formulates a new basis for studying resemblances: "I have been making groups of men and women and grouping the being in them in relation to ambition, to succeeding, to failing in them" (MOA, 663). A number of early portraits present individual variations of the motifs "succeeding" or "failing in living," which also recur in the second half of the Alfred Hersland chapter. Some, including "Five or Six Men," "A Kind of Women," and "Four Protégés," are group portraits; like the descriptions in the novel, they all use a common lexicon that links individuals to paradigms:

> Four certainly are not going to be succeeding in living, not really succeeding in living. Four certainly are not going to be really succeeding in living. Four are ones some one has been selecting to be ones succeeding in living. Certainly these are

ones who are not going to be succeeding in living. ("Four Protégés," T, 305)

Some are ones being very successful ones in being ones being
living. . . .
    One of such of them was one being certainly a very suc-
cessful one in being one being living. This one certainly was
knowing very well that that one was not liking it at all knowing any one who was one not a successful one in being one
being living. This one certainly was loving one and that one
certainly was one not succeeding in being a successful one in
being one being living. . . . This one certainly was knowing
that the one loving him, the one he was marrying then was one
who was completely a successful one. ("Julia Marlowe," T,
328)

He had been one succeeding quite well in living, he was one
succeeding very well in living, he was one going to be succeeding in living. He was one sacrificing succeeding in living
to be one completely living. He certainly was sacrificing and
would be sacrificing succeeding in living to be one completely
living. He was succeeding in living, he had been succeeding in
living, he would be succeeding in living. ("Purrman," T, 334)

In the first and third passages, the various tense formations of the
motif "succeeding in living" ("going to be . . . was . . . had been
. . . would be succeeding in living") signify a more dynamic temporal process than the adjectival formula ("being a successful one")
used in the second. This syntactical sleight-of-hand does not entirely conceal the face that both formulations are based on the same
kind of classification of unchanging "being" that dominates the
novel. Still, this series of portraits employs variations of the motif
"succeeding in living" in combination with a very small number of
other lexical elements to differentiate various interactions between
ambition and achievement, which produce different kinds of tensions within individuals or in their relationships with others.
    In Stein's 1938 study of Picasso, she wrote that the painter
"showed himself to be a great colorist" for the first time during

what she called his "grey period," the years between 1910 and
1912 when he was producing his most austere cubist canvases:
"There is an infinite variety of grey in these pictures and by the
vitality of painting the greys really become color" (P, 45). During
this time Picasso restricted his palette to shades of gray and ocher.
The lexicon of Stein's early portraits, written during the same period, is similarly limited, to the pronouns "one" and "some," occasional adjectives, and the all-pervasive progressive verb forms.
Transitive verbs have as their objects "a thing" or "something,"
not specific concrete nouns. Nothing distracts attention from patterns of action the portraits present. Stein used this restricted lexicon to create a surprising richness of signification. Slight variations
in syntax, tense formation, and word order convey subtle distinc-
tions in meaning. The patterning of sound equivalences and repetitions produces a heightened surface texture that both asserts its
own poetic qualities and creates a network of semantic associations, independent of syntax. And the rhythmic structures of the
prose enact the rhythms of recurrence that characterize their subjects.

The "succeeding in living" series demonstrates the degree of
individual variations in meaning that Stein could produce from
drastically limited semantic resources. But the common lexicon of
these portraits tends to overwhelm the subtleties of individual difference with the force of its dreary sameness. During the summer of
1909, Picasso painted a series of portraits, each more severely reductive than the last. By the end of the series, the individuality of the
subject is obliterated, her head and shoulders reduced to a formal
geometrical structure of intersecting, faceted planes.[3] His portraits
of 1910 and 1911 break the closed form into a far more complex
structure of intersecting facets, which serve as the compositional
scaffolding for the entire canvas. Many of these portraits, especially those of women, are presented as studies of anonymous human form. But in the 1910 portraits of Vollard, Kahnweiler, and
Uhde, which designate their subjects, Picasso supplemented his
austere vocabulary of geometric forms with a few clearly recog-
nizable iconic details to create what Edward Fry has called an
"astonishing likeness" of their subjects.[4] In Kahnweiler's portrait,

the subject's hair, eyebrows, hands, and mouth, as well as a bottle and an African mask on the wall, are clear iconic signs that help the viewer to perceive the entire composition as a legible image.

The most successful of Stein's early portraits also depart from the all-pervasive lexicon of her system to render her subjects' individual patterns of specific actions. A few of them tell stories. "Storyette H.M." is a pointed anecdote about Matisse and his wife, as its title suggests. Repeated rhyming verbs establish the situation: "going off alone to have a good time," he was "glowing"; his wife, left at home to take care of the family, was not. This stripped-down anecdote makes witty use of direct speech to reveal the husband's egotistical domination of his wife: "I am content, you are not content, I am content, you are not content, I am content, you are content, you are content, I am content" (PP, 40). This is the only portrait that quotes direct speech or narrates specific events. "Miss Furr and Miss Skeene," one of Stein's most engaging portraits, is a linear narrative, but, like "Ada," it has motifs of repeated actions embedded in its temporal progression (GP, 17–22). Helen Furr leaves home and begins living with Georgine Skeene. Both are "being gay" and "cultivating their voices." "Being gay," the dominant motif, is repeated with variations that multiply its meanings as the text progresses. When the two women are living together, they are both "regular in being gay," but Miss Skeene is "regular in being a gay one who was one not being gay longer than was needed to be one being quite a gay one." This distinction between the continuing state of "being a gay one" and "being gay," a specific action with more narrowly defined temporal limits, is developed more specifically three paragraphs later:

> To be regularly gay was to do every day the gay thing that they did every day. To be regularly gay was to end every day at the same time after they had been regularly gay. They were regularly gay. They were gay every day. They ended every day in the same way, at the same time, and they had been every day regularly gay. (GP, 18)

The system of internal rhymes linking "gay" to "every day" and to "way" in this passage runs through the entire piece. Emphasized by this excessive singsong rhyme that persistently connects these words, "being gay" comes to signify both a particular action and a statement of sexual identity. After the major event of the story, when Miss Skeene moves out and leaves Miss Furr alone, Miss Furr goes on "being gay." The repetition of this motif, in combination with new secondary motifs of action, subtly and effectively portrays the resulting changes in her life. When the two women are together, they are both "cultivating their voices" and "cultivating in themselves something. . . . They did then learn many ways to be gay." After Miss Furr is left alone, she stops "cultivating her voice" and begins to cultivate her "gayness" more deliberately. "Learning little things to use in being gay" and "telling about learning other ways in being gay" become her major activities. Finally, after she "had used every way to be gay," she "taught very many then little ways they could use in being gay." By the end of the piece, she has become a sad figure, lonely and jaded, reduced to "telling . . . again and again" the finite number of "ways to be gay."[5] In "Miss Furr and Miss Skeene," the interplay of repetition and difference subtly renders a process of psychological change. In the vast majority of Stein's portraits, however, the characters "are what they are. They have not been changing" (PP, 57). Instead of narrating a linear sequence of actions, most of these texts focus exclusively on rendering the continuity of personality that reveals itself in repeated actions.

When Stein began explicating her theory of personality in *The Making of Americans*, she based her understanding on observing the repetition that manifested itself "in ways of eating, in ways of drinking, in ways of loving, in ways of letting anger come out from them about little things in their daily living, in ways of sleeping, in ways of doctoring, . . . ways of thinking, ways of working, ways of beginning, ways of ending, ways of believing" (MOA, 151). As she went on, however, her method of rendering "being" became increasingly detached from its original grounding in patterns of behavior. In "The Gradual Making of *The Making of Americans*," Stein recalled that her desire to render nothing but her synchronic understanding of character forced her to ignore the gradual process of observation that led to her conclusions:

When I was up against the difficulty of putting down the complete conception that I had of an individual, the complete rhythm of a personality that I had gradually acquired by listening seeing feeling and experience, I was faced by the trouble that I had acquired all this knowledge gradually but when I had it I had it completely at one time. . . . And a great deal of The Making of Americans was a struggle to do this thing, to make a whole present of something that it had taken a great deal of time to find out, but it was a whole there then within me and as such it had to be said. (LIA, 147)

The second part of the Alfred Hersland chapter reveals how difficult it was for her to shift her focus from static "being" back to "ways of living": "I am haltingly learning beginning learning this thing, I am remembering how each kind of way of living was a thing not real and having been needing that I should be convincing myself that it really was really an existing way of really living. . . . I know ways of living are repeating, I am not realising them as repeating" (MOA, 621). In the novel, this new interest in "ways of living" only generates more labels and lists, as the author continues her efforts to systematize her knowledge. In the early portraits, she relinquished this demand for "completed understanding," which motivated the totally static descriptive methods she developed in the novel, and created dynamic iconic models of the process of coming to know an individual by observing recurring patterns of action. Instead of repeating the author's conclusions, these texts encourage the reader to participate in the process of understanding. As repetition gradually establishes a network of interconnected motifs, the reader begins to perceive patterns of actions that deepen in significance as the text progresses. The best of these portraits create a more "direct relationship to the object" than literature normally achieves. Reducing to a minumum their lexical resources, they activate syntax, sound, and rhythm to create genuinely iconic models of the objects they portray. The words that name specific actions are arbitrary symbols, but their dense patterning embodies the repetition that is the basis of Stein's theory of personality. The patterns that these rhythms of recurrence gradually create, which "realize" their objects materially as well as symbolically, are literally "present to our feeling" as we read these texts.

While she was writing the Alfred Hersland chapter of *The Making of Americans*, Stein began to crave an audience that could validate the truth of her descriptions of characters. In the novel, her expressed desire "to have every one know every one so that each one could see the meaning of my explanation" is an impossible dream. Even if "every one knew every one," the anonymity and generality of her methods of presentation totally deny the possibility of judging the accuracy of her individual descriptions. Many of her early portraits are equally anonymous. Like painted portraits of unnamed models, they are individualized, but they present themselves as autonomous works of art, independent of any reference to their original subjects. In 1911, however, Stein wrote a series of portraits of artists which invite the reader to evaluate them as likenesses of their subjects.[6] These texts incisively render the patterns of action that characterize each artist's creative processes. Like the other early portraits, their lexicon is strictly limited. Although they do not describe the products of the artists' creative activities in any detail, they still convey acute judgments of their work. Within the series, a number of similar motifs recur. Inviting comparisons and contrasts among the artists portrayed, this recurrence enriches the significance of each motif by highlighting the internal differences within the group. Michael Hoffman has observed, "We must obviously depend on our external knowledge of the subject to make sense out of the writing. We would not even know from the portrait that Picasso was a painter."[7] In fact, these potraits "make sense" even without this knowledge. Like all portraits of well-known subjects, however, they court recognition. The more we know of their subjects, the better we can appreciate their subtleties. The particular lack of specificity that Hoffman describes was essential to Stein's purposes. She was interested in these men as artists whose work raised fundamental aesthetic questions that transcend the boundaries of a single medium. Her understanding of their aesthetic goals and their working methods helped her to formulate her own. Because she regarded these painters as colleagues and potential models in a common exploration of new methods of representation, her portraits of them are richly interesting reflections on some of the crucial aesthetic issues that concerned her at that time.

Stein's notebooks frequently record the raw material of observation and analysis that she used as the point of departure for writing these portraits. She never gave up the habit of using adjectives and abstract nouns to label her analytical insights in her notebooks. In composing the portraits, she transformed these substantive conclusions into dynamic processes, just as she had systematically translated *Q.E.D.*'s abstract nouns into "Melanctha"'s gerundival forms a few years before. A brief comment on Manguin, a minor fauvist painter, typifies the analytical style Stein used in her notebooks: "The sensibility of a light kind and the serious worldliness the idea of pousser of finish of completeness. He can now pousser. He has lost all sensibility" (NB, fragment #22). In the portrait "Manguin a Painter," a "sensibility of a light kind" is suggested by the phrase "making a pretty thing." Variations of the motif "finishing a thing" cleverly render the subject's "serious worldliness the idea of pousser of finish of completeness":

> To finish a thing so that any one can see that that thing is a finished thing is what some one, who is coming to be one finishing something so that any one sees that the thing is a finished thing and who has not been finishing anything so that any one can see that it is a finished thing, is certain is something. (PP, 54)

By the end of the portrait, he "finished everything he was making." Stein's *Making of Americans*, in contrast, is far from a conventionally "finished thing." Constantly foregrounding the continuous, arduous process of writing, that long and difficult text systematically violates the unity and closure of the conventional work of art. In *A Long Gay Book* and a number of other works Stein began while she was writing the novel, the activity of writing is equally dominant. Like *The Making of Americans*, they trace a process of stylistic and epistemological change. Compared to these texts, the portraits are "finished," in their stylistic and thematic unity. As their author acknowledges in "Manguin a Painter," merely "finishing a thing" is "something." Within the series of portraits of artists, however, Manguin's success is hardly impressive, compared to the heroic labor of "greatly expressing something being struggling" that is thematized in "Matisse" (PP, 15).

"Nadelman" (PP, 51–53) portrays an artist whose work was informed by loftier ideals than Manguin's. Several motifs, all of which use the word "light," interact to present an incisive portrait of a man whose sensibility and artistic goals exceed his capacity to fulfill them in his work. The dominant recurring actions in the piece are "feeling light being existing," "thinking about expressing light being existing," and "not expressing light being existing." As a personality, he "had light coming out of him," but he never fully expressed it in his work. The manuscript of the portrait reveals that this motif was first introduced as a concrete description of his ashblonde hair:

> He was one who had very much ~~hair~~ light coming out of him, ~~out of his hair, out of him~~, it came out of him.[8]

In Stein's notebooks, too, fire imagery describes the quality of his sensibility: "[I]n Nadelman there is the steady brilliant inside flame" (NB-E, 2). In the finished portrait, the repeated word "light" is used as a suggestive symbol linking his personality and his artistic endeavors. Nadelman was a sculptor who polished his marble statues to create unusually glossy, crystalline surfaces. In her notebooks, Stein observed, "Nadelman exalted the light [which] would be glad to bathe itself in his statues" (NB-C, 27). In 1912 Nadelman himself wrote,

> A true work of art is created by space, by air and by light as much as by the human heart and soul. If the work of art is not in harmony with exterior elements it remains mediocre. And the function of art is to have the strength and taste to appropriate to itself elements of the exterior world, to bind them to its essence in order to allow them to reflect the grandeur of the world.[9]

In his recent book *Elie Nadelman*, Lincoln Kirstein waxes poetic in his description of the polished surfaces of Nadelman's statues: "Under Nadelman's glassy buffing, contours and volumes fuse, approaching the irreducible primordial egg. Here lurks subtle provocation. His polish is ivory more than ice. Crystalline gloss, vibrating with reflected lights, traps a metaphor of cold flesh, warmed less by blood than cool fire" (p. 181). Kirstein notes that the "cosmetic texture" of Nadelman's work has not been universally admired. The icy perfection of his female heads, with their idealized formal beauty, is devoid of erotic energy. (In 1911, Helena Rubenstein bought the entire contents of an exhibition of his works, to grace her beauty salons.) Stein's portrait presents "expressing being one completely loving women" and "expressing light being existing" as Nadelman's twin aspirations and firmly reiterates the judgment that he never fulfilled either one in his work.

The portrait suggests that Nadelman's failure to achieve his aspirations stems from the predominance of "thinking" over "feeling" in his creative process. From the beginning, the artist is credited with "sensitive feelings"—with "feeling light being existing" and "needing to be one completely loving women." As the text gradually develops its interconnected motifs, however, it soon reveals that "thinking," detached from "feeling," governs his artistic production. Early in the portrait, he is "completely working" and "completely thinking about expressing light being existing." By the end, he is presented in terms that make clear the nature of his failure:

> This one was one expressing thinking, this one was one expressing complete working. This one was one not expressing completely loving women. This one was one having some light coming out of him. This one was one not expressing light being existing.

Stein's limited lexicon powerfully underscores the connection, as well as the gulf, between "completely thinking about expressing light being existing" and expressing nothing but "thinking." Nadelman interested Stein greatly for a short time. In 1908 she and her brother bought a number of his drawings and a curious statue, modeled on Praxiteles' Aphrodite, which portrays Stein's face and figure. As early as 1905, Nadelman began creating drawings that reduce the human anatomy to curvilinear forms. His sculptures, frequently based on Greek models, demonstrate a similar, but less radical, geometrical reduction. In 1910 he wrote, "But what is the form of art? It is significant and abstract: i.e., composed of geometrical elements."[10] André Salmon's 1914 review of Nadelman's work characterizes the artist as "above all, a theorist, a theorist in spite of himself," and adds, "Let us not forget that Nadelman sacrificed everything to the relations of volumes a long time before the Cubists."[11] By the time she wrote his portrait, Stein was clearly disenchanted with Nadelman's penchant for theory. The relationship between sensibility and intellect in the creative process is a recurring concern in Stein's notebook analyses of artists. And the interplay of "thinking" and "feeling" that dominates Nadelman's portrait is a prominent theme in a number of other texts Stein wrote in 1911, including the David Hersland chapter of the novel and *Two*.

Stein's portraits of Picasso and Matisse, which first appeared as companion pieces in the August 1912 issue of *Camera Work*, characterize their subjects not only as individual personalities and working artists but also in their public roles as leaders in the art world. Picasso is "one whom some are certainly following" (PP, 17–20). "Some said of [Matisse], when anybody believed in him they did not then believe in any other one" (PP, 12–16). For knowing readers of this influential American art journal, the mere juxtaposition of these two artists, whose work had begun to develop in radically different directions a few years before, would have evoked the recent conflict between their divergent aesthetics, which had split the French avant-garde into two distinct camps. In the two years after the Steins bought their first Matisse painting, *Woman with the Hat*, with its brilliant, riotous colors that shocked the public and the critics at the 1905 Salon d'automne, Matisse won public recognition as leader of the fauves and as the most influential younger master in Paris. By 1907, however, Picasso's work had seriously challenged Matisse's leadership of the avant-garde. Although not shown publicly until many years later, *Les Demoiselles d'Avignon* and Picasso's subsequent reinterpretations of Cézanne interested many young painters more powerfully than Matisse's recent work. Coincidentally, at the time Cézanne's work began to come into vogue after his death in 1906, Matisse, who had been studying Cézanne's paintings for a number of years and adapting some of his techniques, began to pursue a different direction. In his 1907 *Blue Still-life*, he was still masterfully rendering solid forms in deep space, from a Cézannesque high perspective. After 1907, however, his paintings increasingly subordinate three-dimensional volume to all-over decorative patterning.[12] In *Harmony in Blue* (1908) and *Harmony in Red* (1909), the monochromatic arabesques of the tablecloths are repeated in the background. This purely decorative two-dimensional figure dominates the canvas. Although Matisse's international reputation increased rapidly beginning in 1908, he lost his position of leadership among Parisian painters. In 1907 and 1908 several of the artists who were first recognized as fauvist painters, including Vlaminck, Derain, and Braque, became more interested in reinterpreting Cézanne and exploring Picasso's innovative treatment of three-dimensional space than in following the direction of Matisse's latest work. In 1907 Braque was an exciting new fauvist painter. In 1908 he submitted his early cubist landscapes to the Salon d'automne. Matisse was a member of the jury that refused them.

"Matisse" thematizes some of the issues involved in this shift of allegiances. Stein observed this drama of defection at close range; indeed, she was one of the defectors. Since 1905 the entire Stein family—Gertrude and Leo, their elder brother Michael, and his wife Sarah—had been Matisse's patrons and close friends.[13] Gertrude and Leo Stein both disliked Matisse's new style; after 1907 they bought no more of his paintings. In her 1909 notebooks, Stein wrote: "He must paint after nature, his in between decorative period was and is a failure, it is only carried by his beautiful colors and his power in drawing but they have no real existence. He has always failed in such flat painting, he then of course not understanding his own failure cannot understand Pablo who succeeds in just this" (NB-A, 13). Her portrait of Matisse is an acute study of the artist, based on her intimate knowledge of his personality, his paintings, and his theories of art. Because the controversy it presents was crucial to Stein's definition of her own aesthetic stance, "Matisse" is her richest and most complex exploration of the fundamental premises that governed her own work at this time.

"Matisse" begins with the artist's agonizing uncertainty:

> One was quite certain that for a long part of his being one being living he had been trying to be certain that he was wrong in doing what he was doing and then when he could not come to be certain that he had been wrong in doing what he had been doing, when he had completely convinced himself that he would not come to be certain that he had been wrong in doing what he had been doing he was really certain then that he was a great one and he certainly was a great one. Certainly every one could be certain of this thing that this one is a great one.

Stein's notebooks record the source of the insight that she transformed into the long opening sentence: "Matisse Sally was saying and it probably came from him, Matisse spent eight years trying to prove to himself that he was wrong, of a Cezanne one would always say that he was trying to prove to himself that he was right" (NB-H, 4). In the portrait, the convoluted syntax of the indirect discourse models Matisse's tortuous questioning of his work, the arduous resistance that only gradually yields to certainty. Repetition of the word "certain" in three different contexts charges the indirect discourse with ironic tension. At the end of the sentence, direct authorial statement confirms the artist's hard-won certainty: "and he certainly was a great one. Certainly every one could be certain of this thing that this one is a great one." Beginning in the third paragraph, a dialogical interplay of conflicting "certainties" portrays the range of critical judgments of Matisse's work. As indirect statements, each introduced by the phrase "some were certain," assert their mutually contradictory opinions, this incessant verbal repetition begins to resemble the characters' increasingly futile search for certainty in "Melanctha." Throughout this text, however, direct authorial statement frequently intervenes, as it does at the end of the first paragraph, to assert the authority of its own certainty in the midst of this flurry of competing truths.

The third paragraph inaugurates the critical controversy with the direct statement, "He certainly very clearly expressed something." Although a variety of conflicting opinions immediately follow, "clearly expressing something" emerges as the central motif in Matisse's portrait, consistently validated by authorial certainty. This motif economically condenses the two major themes that dominate Stein's analysis of Matisse in her notebooks and the painter's own statements of his aesthetic principles as well. In "Notes d'un peintre," first published in 1908, he insists, again and again, that "expression of his feeling" is his essential concern:

> What I am after, above all, is expression. . . . I am unable to distinguish between the feeling I have for life and my way of expressing it.
>
> Expression to my way of thinking does not consist of the passion mirrored upon a human face or betrayed by a violent gesture. The whole arrangement of my picture is expressive. The place occupied by figures or objects, the empty spaces around them, the proportions, everything plays a part. *Composition is the art of arranging in a decorative manner the various elements at the painter's disposal for the expression of his feelings.*[14]

Stein's notebooks emphasize this primacy of emotional expression in Matisse's art. The accuracy of her description of him as a "practical realist," who works "not from [Cézanne's and Picasso's] immediate contact with the object but from a passionate emotion about the object," is confirmed by a comment Sarah Stein recorded in her notes from his 1908 painting classes: "To copy the objects in a still life is nothing; one must render the emotion they awaken in him. . . . The tear-like quality of this slender, fat-bellied vase—the generous volume of this copper—must touch you."[15]

Stein's notebook analysis of Matisse also emphasizes the emotional and expressive clarity of his work: "Matisse is clear in his emotional power, that has a clarity and pushes through all obstacles and the more the resistance, the difficulties the more vivid the expression. . . . Matisse has cleanness as an intellectual pictorial quality" (NB-H, 4, 3). This characterization echoes the second major theme of Matisse's 1908 essay:

> For me all is in the conception—I must have a clear vision of the whole composition from the very beginning. I could mention the name of a great sculptor who produces some admirable pieces but for him a composition is nothing but a grouping of fragments and the result is a confusion of expression. Look instead at one of Cézanne's pictures: all is so well arranged in them that no matter how many figures are represented and no matter at what distance you stand, you will be able always to distinguish each figure clearly and you will always know which limb belongs to which body. *If in the picture there is order and clarity it means that this same order and clarity existed in the mind of the painter and that the painter was conscious of their necessity.* Limbs may cross, may mingle, but still in the eyes of the beholder they will remain attached to the right body. All confusion will have disappeared.[16]

During the same year that Matisse invoked Cézanne's paintings as models of his own ideal of "order and clarity," Picasso and Braque were departing from their own reinterpretation of Cézanne (truly "le père de nous tous") to create the deliberately disordered, fragmented images of "analytical" cubism. Stein's portrait of Matisse uses the motif "greatly expressing something being struggling" to signify the aesthetic stance that emerged to challenge the supreme value of clear expression:

> He certainly very clearly expressed something. Some said that he did not clearly express anything. Some were certain that he expressed something very clearly and some of such of them said that he would have been a greater one if he had not been one so clearly expressing what he was expressing. Some said he was not clearly expressing what he was expressing and some of such of them said that the greatness of struggling

which was not clear expression made of him one being a completely great one.

Some said of him that he was greatly expressing something struggling. Some said of him that he was not greatly expressing something struggling.

He certainly was clearly expressing something, certainly sometime any one might come to know that of him.

From the beginning of this debate, the two dominant motifs are presented as mutually exclusive. "Some" immediately call into question the aesthetic value of Matisse's clear expression, while "some" of Matisse's admirers are "certain" that the power of his work derives from the "greatness of struggling which was not clear expression." After two paragraphs rendering this division of opinion, the text reiterates its authoritative judgment: "He certainly was clearly expressing something" and closes this portion of the debate. After this, Matisse's clarity of expression and his greatness are both presented as certainties. The "some" who had doubted this are replaced, in the next paragraph, by the "very many" who "did come to know that of him." Then a new certainty is added: "Certainly he was expressing something being struggling." But the question of whether or not he was "greatly expressing something being struggling" remains unresolved until the sixth paragraph, which finally asserts, "Certainly he was one not greatly expressing something being struggling."

As these authoritative statements gradually emerge from the flood of competing certainties, the author's own allegiance to the aesthetics of struggle becomes increasingly clear. The fifth and sixth paragraphs present the reactions of Matisse's followers, torn between his art of "clearly expressing something" and the challenge of the competing aesthetics. A single long sentence narrates the defection of some of his former disciples:

There were very many who were wanting to be ones doing what he was doing that is to be ones clearly expressing something and *then* very many of them were not wanting to be being ones doing that thing, that is clearly expressing something, they wanted to be ones expressing something being struggling,

something being going to be some other thing, something being going to be something some one sometime would be clearly
expressing and that would be something that would be a thing
then that would then be greatly expressing some other thing
then that thing, certainly very many *were then* not wanting to
be doing what this one was doing clearly expressing something
and some of them *had been* ones wanting to be doing that
thing wanting to be ones clearly expressing something.

Their choice of "greatly expressing something being struggling" is
presented as a radical commitment to art as process, to the continual creation of "something being going to be some other thing,
something being going to be something some one sometime would
be clearly expressing." This revolutionary art does not work from
a prior subject, an already constituted "something" which it pro-
ceeds to express. It is, itself, "something being struggling," which
has an autonomous force that impels further discoveries. Those of
Matisse's followers who reject this challenge and continue "wanting to be ones clearly expressing something" are excluded from this
historical process of collective creation. In contrast to this new aesthetics, the portrait asserts, their clear expression "was in them
a thing not really interesting then any other one."

This portrait never names Picasso as the representative of the
new aesthetics some of Matisse's followers embrace. Their choice,
like the dynamic process of artistic discovery itself, is presented
impersonally, in terms of aesthetic ideals, not men. Still, readers
familiar with this period of art history will recognize Picasso's
painting as the force that galvanized Matisse's former disciples. In
*Picasso*, Stein explicitly attributes to her friend an aesthetic theory
similar to the one that opposes Matisse's clarity of expression in the
early portrait:

Picasso said once that he who created a thing is forced to make
it ugly. In the effort to create the intensity and the struggle to
create this intensity, the result always produces a certain ugliness, those who follow can make of this thing a beautiful thing
because they know what they are doing, the thing having already been invented, but the inventor because he does not

know what he is going to invent inevitably the thing he makes must have its ugliness. (P, 9)

In this formulation, beauty is sacrificed in the arduous struggle of creating genuinely new forms; in the portrait of Matisse, it is clarity. Stein's readers will recognize her own dedication to this aesthetics of struggle, with its rejection of conventional beauty and clarity and its continual pursuit of innovation. The form of Matisse's portrait itself demonstrates her own refusal of conventionally clear expression. Like all of her early texts, it illustrates her continuing struggle to invent new forms.

In *The Making of Americans*, Stein constantly thematizes her own agonizing labors, confessing all her frustrations and anxieties, as if the extremity of her personal suffering would guarantee the intensity of the work of art. In the Matisse portrait, however, she firmly denies any necessary connection between the personal struggle of creation and the work that is the autonomous expression of *"something* being struggling." The portrait begins and ends with Matisse's tortuous self-doubt. The long first sentence that begins paragraph 8 repeats a variation of the process of agonizing questioning presented in the first paragraph and then concludes, "this then made him certain this, that he would always be one being suffering, this made him certain that he was expressing something being struggling, and certainly very many were quite certain that he was greatly expressing something being struggling." Throughout the second half of the portrait, the compelling rhythms of repetition portray Matisse endlessly complaining of his suffering and his acquaintances, subjected to "hearing it again and again," reiterating their judgments of his work. This section of the portrait seems to parody the author's incessant laments in *The Making of Americans*, reminding us that a confessional "I" whose struggles dominate the novel is absent from the portraits. In this portrait, the artist's "telling very often about being one suffering" convinces many listeners that his art expresses "something being struggling," but the text never validates this judgment with the authority of direct statement. Indeed, as "Notes d'un peintre" clearly reveals, the art Matisse aspired to create was far removed form the arena of his personal struggles: "What I dream of is an art of balance, of purity and serenity devoid of troubling and depressing subject matter, an art which might be for every mental worker, be he businessman or writer, like an appeasing influence, like a mental soother, something like a good armchair in which to rest from physical fatigue."[17] Although Stein's portrait never deviates from its judgment that Matisse is a "great one," it strongly suggests that, for all his personal suffering, he never produced the truly seminal works, fraught with dynamic internal tensions, that she valued most highly.

In her notebooks, Stein wrote, "Not express yourself like Matisse but be giving birth like Cezanne and Picasso and me" (NB, fragment #130). "Picasso" (PP, 17–20), less solemn than "Matisse," is a celebration of her friend's fecund creativity. Its central motif is a passive construction, "something was coming out of him," which suggests that his work, the grammatical subject, has a force of its own, independent of the artist's intentional control. Stein's portrait of Picasso is more playful and more lyrical than her presentation of Matisse's arduous "suffering" or Nadelman's laborious "thinking." Beginning with the first sentence, "One whom some were certainly following was one who was completely charming," repeating rhythmical figures, reinforced by assonance, consonance, and rhyme, create a lilting, melodic effect. The prose rhythms of this portrait are completely different from those of "Matisse." Its sentences, shorter and syntactically less complex than those used to characterize Matisse, are frequently broken into long series of short noun phrases. Their quick, nervous rhythms are strikingly different from the long, slowly revolving sentences in "Matisse." The contrast between the tortuous hesitation and self-doubt modeled in the long, convoluted sentences of "Matisse" and the effortless outpouring of genius portrayed in the simple sentences of "Picasso" delineates a fundamental difference between the two artists. The acuity of this contrast is confirmed by Picasso's later comment on Matisse's working methods: "Matisse makes a drawing, then he makes a copy of it. He recopies it five times, ten times, always clarifying the line. He's convinced that the last, the most stripped down, is the best, the purest, the definitive one: and in fact, most of the time, it was the first. In drawing, nothing is better than the first attempt."[18]

Like "Matisse," "Picasso" presents a view of the artist that encompasses his public position as well as the individual quality of his creativity. In the latter, however, the opinions of "some," limited to those who are "certainly following" Picasso, express unanimous praise, not the wider range of critical judgments presented in "Matisse." Direct authorial statement corrects their excessively solemn, awestruck vision of their master. While his charmed followers are "certain that the one they were then following was one *bringing out* of himself then something that was coming to be a heavy thing, a solid thing and a complete thing," the authorial voice immediately counters this active formulation of the artist's creative processes by reiterating its own passive construction, "having something coming out of him," which becomes the dominant motif of the portrait. In contrast to the weightiness and consistency the followers see in Picasso's work ("a heavy thing, a solid thing and a complete thing"), the text later proposes another description that explodes the coherence of the first:

> This one always had something being coming out of this one. This one was working. This one always had been working. This one was always having something that was coming out of this one that was a solid thing, a charming thing, a lovely thing, a perplexing thing, a disconcerting thing, a simple thing, a clear thing, a complicated thing, an interesting thing, a disturbing thing, a repellant thing, a very pretty thing.

The repeating syntactical pattern emphasizes the logical disarray of this bewildering catalogue of descriptive adjectives. "Simple" and "clear" are placed in direct opposition to "complicated" and "perplexing"; "very pretty" is starkly juxtaposed to "repellant." The irregular rhythm of the short phrases and the singsong repetition of the word "thing" heighten the sense of logical incoherence. But, in fact, the paintings Picasso produced between 1905 and 1911 encompass the full range of qualities described in this wildly diverse list of adjectives: the "very pretty," "charming" iconography of his rose period; *Les Demoiselles d'Avignon*, "disturbing" and "repellant" at first, even to his most fervent admirers; the "clear" Cézannesque landscapes and still lifes of 1908; the "solid" landscapes and heads painted in 1909; and, most recently, the "perplexing," "complicated" iconography of the 1910–11 portraits and landscapes. The deliberately chaotic arrangement of this series of adjectives, which defies logical or chronological ordering, emphasizes the unusual degree of eclectic stylistic experimentation that characterized Picasso's entire career. Another, equally chaotic set of adjectives functions similarly, to demonstrate the impossibility of locating a single, consistent "meaning" in Picasso's fecund production: "Something had been coming out of him, certainly it had been coming out of him, certainly it was something, certainly it had been coming out of him and it had meaning, a charming meaning, a solid meaning, a struggling meaning, a clear meaning." Both of these passages present the continuing force of his creativity as the only consistent characteristic of his work. Later, the portrait suggests that this incessant activity is an end in itself: "This one was working and then this one was working and this one was needing to be working, not to be one having something coming out of him something having meaning, but was needing to be working so as to be one working." Unmotivated by any particular desire for self-expression or communication, "This one was not working to have anything come out of him." The latter part of the portrait reiterates the judgment that he "was not completely working." But despite his lack of complete concentration and of any intention to create a specific meaning, the portrait insists, "The thing coming out of him always had a complete meaning."

I have presented this explication of "Picasso" without referring to Stein's notebooks, to demonstrate that these texts have a "real meaning" that is accessible to any attentive reader, once he understands their process of signification. At this point, a passage from Stein's notebook, which clearly reveals the meaning she intended to communicate in this portrait, will emphasize how deliberately she manipulated her limited lexicon, activating the resources of syntax, sound, and rhythm in the service of signification:

Do one about Pablo his emotional leap and courage as opposed to lack of courage in Cezanne and me. *His laziness and
his lack of continuity and his facility too quick for the content
which ought to be so complete to do what he wants to do.* His
work is not because it is too strong for him to resist but because
his resistance is not great enough. Cezanne resistance great but
dragged along. Pablo is never dragged, he walks in the light,
and a little ahead of himself like Raphael, therefore his things
often lack a base. Do him.

    One whom some were certainly following was one who
was completely charming. (NB-13, 14; my emphasis)

Syntactical structures model her sense of the "leaps" and discon-
tinuities in Picasso's career, as well as the facility of his working methods. Sound and syntax work together to create the nervous, broken rhythms of this portrait, so different from the slow,
sonorous movement of the sentences in "Matisse." In her notebooks, Stein frequently characterized Matisse as "slow"; in contrast, she described Picasso as "nervously energized into rapid action" (NB, fragment #41; E, 12). Beginning in *Q.E.D.*, Stein was
working with the idea that fundamental personality differences revealed themselves in different rhythms of response: the two lovers'
"pulses were differently timed" (QED, 104). In "The Good Anna,"
she used contrasting speech rhythms to illustrate the differences between Anna's nervous energy and Mrs. Lehntman's slower, more
lethargic temperament. "Melanctha" and *The Making of Americans* both thematize these contrasting rhythms of response, but the
prose rhythms of both of these texts are uniformly slow. The long,
complex sentences of *The Making of Americans* model the slowly
revolving thought processes of the author (who characterized herself, like Matisse, as slow), not the individual rhythms of the characters they attempt to describe.

    The portraits are an elegant solution to the problem of "realiz-
ing" individual characters in dynamic literary form. Rather than
labeling the rhythms of personality that characterize these subjects,
they inscribe them in the material patterning of the texts. These

individual rhythmic figures, combined with the all-pervasive repetition that enacts the recurrence of characterizing actions, both reinforce and supplement lexical meaning. The rhythmic virtuosity of
"Orta or One Dancing" totally fuses lexical meaning and iconic
figuration:

> In dancing she was dancing. She was dancing and dancing
> and in being that one the one dancing and dancing she was
> dancing and dancing. In dancing, dancing being existing, she
> was dancing, and in being one dancing dancing was being ex-
> isting.
>      She was one and being one she was one in a way being
> one, she was one dancing. She was one she was one dancing.
> She was one dancing, she was being one, she was in a way one,
> she was one, she was one dancing. (T, 302)

Throughout this portrait of Isadora Duncan, the dancer and her
dancing are powerfully rendered in the rhythmic play of signifiers
that enacts the shifting measures of the dance.

The exuberantly varied rhythm of this text, more like the rapid, broken rhythms of "Picasso" than the ponderous movement of
The Making of Americans and "Matisse," signals a new direction
in Stein's writing. As the preceding quotation from her notebooks
indicates, she had identified her temperament with Matisse's at the
same time she was aligning her aesthetic orientation with Picasso's.
The suffering "I" that dominates The Making of Americans, which
so closely resembles the artistic temperament portrayed in "Matisse," disappeared in the early portraits, but the underlying theory
and analysis of character remained virtually unchanged. She was
still working to translate her prior analytical insights into literary form. Soon after she composed the portraits that starkly contrast Picasso's working methods with Matisse's, she began to cultivate the effortless spontaneity portrayed in "Picasso" in her own
writing. In "Orta" she explored the rhythmic freedom of Isadora
Duncan's dancing in her own medium. In "Play" (PP, 160), she
celebrated another form of liberation from the arduous creative
struggles dramatized in the early chapters of The Making of Ameri-

*cans.* Two longer texts, the David Hersland chapter of the novel and *Two*, delineate Stein's gradual abandonment of the portrait style and its underlying epistemological assumptions in favor of a more spontaneous mode of writing, in which she no longer worked so consciously or deliberately "to be one having something coming out of [her] something having meaning."

"The Complete Connection":
*Two* and Other Transitional Texts

$\int$ TEIN resumed work on *The Making of
Americans* in the autumn of 1911. In less than two months, she
completed the last two hundred pages of the novel, using the new
method of representation she had perfected in the short portraits
she had written during the previous year. In the opening pages of
the David Hersland chapter, the authorial "I" is still struggling to
defend her universal system of classification against the threat of
her own growing uncertainty. But this dramatized quest for "completed understanding" of "kinds" soon cedes to a third-person rendering of the life and death of David Hersland in the style of the
early portraits. In the course of writing this chapter, however, Stein
began to call into question the validity of all totalizing systems of
knowledge, including the unified, synoptic analysis of personality
that informed the method of the portraits. Before the end of *The
Making of Americans*, she was paradoxically using this style to
deny its most fundamental premises. This process of questioning
continued in *Two*, which Stein began while she was working on the
final sections of the novel. Like the David Hersland chapter, it
begins in the style of the early portraits and gradually undermines
its underlying assumptions. Stein conceived of this text as a study
contrasting her brother Leo's analytical habits of mind with her
sister-in-law Sally's more spontaneous, intuitive responses. While
exploring the opposition between these two ways of processing experience, Stein reversed her own epistemological stance. Before she
completed the novel, she had already abandoned her goal of sys-
tematized understanding. In *Two* she began to develop a new style
to model the rich diversity of experience unmediated by rational
analysis.

While she was working on these two projects, Stein became
preoccupied with the question of "how each one is experiencing,

with what feeling, thinking, believing, creating" (MOA, 729). In the David Hersland chapter of the novel, "realis[ing] the experiencing in each one" replaces "realising" individual "being" as the author's central concern. Early in the chapter, the authorial "I" confesses how difficult it is for her to account for "the way each one is experiencing each thing" (737). Later it is David Hersland who was "not realising very well which way any one was experiencing anything and the relation of doing thinking in each one doing thinking with the way each one is experiencing" (770). With this merger of the author's interests with the character's, the discursive "I" disappears, leaving David Hersland as its surrogate. From the beginning of the novel, Stein had conceived of this character as its hero: "But there is still some hope for us in the younger David who is different from the people all around us, in him who always was seeking to be free inside him, to know it in him, and no one could ever understand him, what it was inside him that made it right that he should go on with his living" (48). Stein's 1908 notebooks record her intention to use this character to portray her own development: "Must realise my hero by making him go through my development."[1] In the novel, David Hersland's birth is contingent on the death of two siblings. His parents wanted only three children. If all of them had lived, he would not have been born. This closely parallels the similar contingency of Gertrude and Leo Stein's births. This knowledge made both of them "feel funny," she recalled in *Everybody's Autobiography* (134). In *The Making of Americans*, it results in the hero's "needing to be understanding every minute in being living what meaning there was to him in his needing to be to him one being being living" (743). David Hersland is not simply a version of Gertrude Stein; her notebook analyses of her brother and several other men contributed to her portrayal of this character.[2] But David Hersland's quest for meaning closely resembles that of the authorial "I" before it cedes to this character: "He was one all his living interested in ways of eating, ways of being one going on being in living, in listening, in talking, in dying, in loving" (734). He "came to be one certain sometime to be completely understanding being being in men and in women" (777).

Their shared preoccupation with the question of "how each

one is experiencing" manifests itself in the interplay of "thinking" and "feeling" that pervades the chapter. In contrast to the repeated physical actions of childhood, "jumping" and being "tossed" and learning to "toss" oneself, the characterizing actions of the hero's adult life are purely internal (795, 843). He "said some things and did some things," but this chapter does not narrate anecdotal actions or quote speeches and thoughts (827). Focusing instead on his experience as "one being living to himself inside him," it centers on the particular balance of "thinking" and "feeling" that characterizes his internal life (827). As he matures, David's need for intellectual clarity grows stronger, and he makes a conscious decision to dedicate himself to "completely living in thinking clearly about the things about which he was thinking" (855).

By the time she had reached this point in the novel, Stein herself had concluded that "very clearly thinking" is incompatible with "completely experiencing":

> Many who are carefully and completely thinking have it to leave out something they have been, they will be, they are, they can be experiencing and this is a very natural thinking as very many who have it to be ones clearly and completely reasonably thinking have it to have it that they are thinking to be solving a problem and naturally then they are not thinking into them everything they can be experiencing. Some are quite certain that any one very clearly thinking are not ever completely experiencing, some are quite certain that any one clearly thinking is leaving out very much that should be being remembered by that one. (779–80)

Stein's original plan was to make David the "completed individual."[3] In this chapter, although his intense dedication to "clearly thinking" is his dominant characteristic, it does not prevent him from being concerned with "clearly feeling" and expressing his feelings as well. In contrast to those described in the passage quoted above, who attain intellectual clarity at the price of "leaving out very much that should be being remembered," Stein's hero "was needing for his own satisfaction to put in everything any one could be experiencing in thinking about anything" (780).

At the same time Stein composed this passage, she was writing a long, devastatingly critical analysis of her brother Leo in her notebooks, which was the point of departure for her portrait of him in *Two*.[4] She attributed his failures as an artist and a philosopher to his exclusive dedication to analytical thought, which resulted in a "lack of richness of internal general experience":

> He thinks thinkingly and analytically but he does not present the object to his thought not having the experience. . . . His experiencing power is too limited, for any real originality in creating or philosophizing. . . . [W]hen he makes philosophical discoveries it is with the intellect everything away because I think everything should be away so that I can think the world rational or so the world can be right not putting everything away because it is in the way and you must shove it away to feel it. (NB-M, 26)

Earlier, in the Martha Hersland chapter of the novel, she had written a description of a "kind" of people who are "stultified in their living by running themselves by their minds," which "cuts them off from experiencing" (366–67). In 1911 "experiencing" became her new slogan for creativity: the "only way to unconventionalize is by the power of experiencing" (NB-M, 26). Identifying her brother Leo's failures with his excess of rational control and redefining her own intellectual stance in opposition to his, she began to regard all analytical thought as a barrier to the unmediated experience that nurtures creativity.

William James regarded all conceptions as "teleological instruments" created by the human mind, for its own ends, to impose order on what he called the "concrete chaos" of immediate sensory experience.[5] When her brother Leo strenuously objected, on these grounds, to her methods of describing character in 1909, Stein reacted by declaring her rejection of James's philosophical pragmatism: "When Leo said that all classification was teleological I knew I was not a pragmatist" (NB-D, 11). But even during the time that she was eagerly embracing Otto Weininger's theories and methods of characterology as an alternative intellectual model, she never abandoned her early commitment to James's teachings to the extent of totally accepting the philosophical idealism that was the foundation of Weininger's system. For Weininger, the "conception is . . . the creator of reality. . . . The idea of a standard of truth, the idea of truth, cannot lie in experience."[6] Stein's theories of personality, as she insisted throughout the early chapters of *The Making of Americans*, were always firmly grounded in her own immediate experience of herself and others, in accord with James's axiom, "Introspective Observation is what we have to rely on first and foremost and always" (*Principles*, 1:185).

In her 1911 notebooks, Stein resorted to explicitly Jamesian terminology to describe the quality of her creativity: "Sally when working concentrates her attention, I concentrate myself. . . . All creative people concentrate themselves" (NB-E, 9). According to Jamesian psychology, most of the sensory impressions that flood into the consciousness are filtered out by the faculty of "attention," which functions as a "sieve in which we try to gather up the world's contents. Most facts and relations fall through its meshes, being either too subtle or insignificant to be fixed in any conception" (*Principles*, 1:482). In this way, the "conceiving or theorizing faculty" of the mind transforms the "world of our impressions into a totally different world—the world of our conception."[7] In "Reflex Action and Theism," James argues that the "utter chaos" of immediate sensory experience is the only "real order of the world" and that all the "orders" created by arts and science are equally "subjective" systems imposed on this "real world" to help us feel at home in it. In "The Sentiment of Rationality," he eloquently insists that every conceptual order entails a sacrifice of the "teeming and dramatic vividness of the concrete world": "Simple classification of things is, on the one hand, the best possible theoretic philosophy but is, on the other, a most miserable and inadequate substitute for the fulness of the truth. It is a monstrous abridgment of life, which, like all abridgments, is got by the absolute loss and casting out of real matter" (*Essays*, pp. 70, 69).

Fighting against James's assumption that all systems of classification are subjective orders that the human mind creates for its own ends, Stein began her novel with the faith that her methods of analysis were firmly grounded in the experiential "reality" of repetition. But the more directly the novel reveals the urgency of her need to systematize her experience, the more clearly her project inadvertently confirms the Jamesian hypothesis that "all classification is teleological." Her own craving for order led her to pursue what James called the "abstract monotony" of classification at the expense of all individual diversity in the novel. In the early portraits Stein left behind the descriptive apparatus of *The Making of Americans* but not her reductive theory of personality. Her idea that character is revealed through repeated actions itself functioned as a "sieve" that filtered out everything that did not contribute to her unified conception. In James's terms, the method of the early portraits entailed the same "absolute loss and casting out of real matter" that characterize any theoretical system. In Stein's own terms, she herself had been "leaving out very much that should be being remembered" in her methods of rendering character. The conceptual models that informed her presentation of "being" in the novels and in the portraits were as reductive as the analytical habits of thought she criticized in her brother Leo and others who "run themselves by their minds."

In the David Hersland chapter of the novel she began to confront these striking contradictions between her theories of creativity and the epistemological assumptions governing her methods of representation. Early in the chapter the author confesses her doubts about the possibility of achieving total understanding of human nature. After the authorial "I" disappears from the text, the hero is used to portray Stein's own increasing uncertainty about the validity of her system of classification: "In a way David Hersland did know very well what kind he was of ones experiencing, of ones expressing, in a way he never came to be completely certain that he was not perhaps another kind of a one experiencing, another kind of a one expressing" (MOA, 784). His intellectual stance, which combines "clearly thinking" with "needing . . . to put in everything any one could be experiencing," makes it impossible for him to accept the fundamental premises of the author's methods of representation in the earlier sections of the novel. He is unable to see anything as a "complete thing" (861). At the beginning of the chapter the author reaffirms her belief that people never change

(728). Later, her surrogate "was realising all his living that chang-ing is existing in every one and he was not really feeling this thing, really seeing this thing until the middle of the beginning of his mid-dle living and then he was loving this thing" (844). In radical oppo-sition to the elaborate system of resemblances that dominates the early parts of the novel, David Hersland is "almost certain that any one is different from any other one" (877). Near the end of the chapter, he is described as "one who was completely different from any other one" (901). But the most obvious of all the reversals in this chapter occurs in the flat statement, "He was not really repeat-ing anything, he was clearly not repeating anything" (891).

In this chapter, the operations of the discourse systematically begin to undermine many of the certainties posited earlier in the novel. Repetition is used more often to suggest a wide range of pos-sibilities than to enforce a single truth:

> Certainly some are living and are being ones going on be-ing living and are needing for this thing being certain that being living is having meaning and is being then existing. Cer-tainly some are living and are being ones going on being living and are not troubling and are needing for this thing being cer-tain that being living is having meaning and is being then exist-ing. Certainly some are living and are being ones going on being living and are not troubling and are not needing for this thing being certain that being living is having meaning and is being then existing. Certainly some are living and are going on being living and are troubling and are needing for this thing that being living is having meaning and is being then existing. Certainly some are being living and are going on being living and are troubling and are needing to be certain that being liv-ing is not having meaning, that being living is not existing. Some are being living and are going on being living and are troubling and they are needing that being living is not having any meaning and that being living is existing. (835)

Descriptions of David Hersland frequently use repetition to jux-tapose a series of mutually contradictory assertions, sometimes within a single sentence: "He was one troubling, he was one not troubling, he was one needing that being living is having meaning, he was one needing that being living is existing. He was one troubling, he was one not troubling, he was one needing that being living has not any meaning, he was one needing that being living is not existing" (835–36). These bewildering series model the hero's internal contradictions and ambivalences. Frequent adverbial qualifications ("sometimes," "in a way," "almost completely . . . not completely") disclaim any pretense of portraying his "whole being." Change and difference, the only certainties the hero affirms, are modeled in the syntactical structures of the discourse.

In the earlier sections of the novel, Stein clearly revealed the terror of meaningless fragmentation that impelled her quest for "completed understanding." She needed a totalizing order to create an "everlasting feeling" to combat her fear of senseless mortality. When she began the David Hersland chapter, she experienced her failure to achieve this goal as a kind of death: "I tell you I cannot bear it this thing that I cannot be realising experiencing in each one being living, I say it again and again I cannot let myself be really resting in believing this thing, it is in me now as when I am realising being a dead one, a one being dying and I can do this thing and I do this thing and I am filled then with complete desolation" (729). She went on to create a surrogate hero to preside over the destruction of the order she had tried so desperately to create. From the beginning of the chapter, David Hersland's early death is a foregone conclusion. This stark, reiterated fact dominates the chapter. It is the one overwhelming certainty that unifies the other diverse and contradictory facts of his life. No physical cause of death is ever suggested; he simply "had not been needing being one going on going on being living" (902). After "realising" her hero's death and, with it, the death of her own hopes for achieving "completed understanding," Stein ended her massive novel with a compelling litany that reiterates the only certainty that remained: the universal repetition of the cycle of life and death.

In *Two* Stein directly thematized the opposition between the epistemological stance that governed the early sections of *The*

*Making of Americans* and the radically different one that began to emerge in the David Hersland chapter. In a letter written in February 1912, she characterized this work as a "study of a man and a woman having the same means of expression and the same emotional and spiritual experiences with different qualities of intellect."[8] The Yale edition of *Two* subtitles it *Gertrude Stein and Her Brother*, but manuscript notes reveal that its original subjects were her brother Leo and her sister-in-law Sally. Stein had analyzed both of them in her notebooks and concluded that they were equally deficient as creative personalities, for opposite reasons. Leo's excess of rationality separates him from immediate experience. Sally is "more capable of first hand experience from sensitiveness but with that her intellect does not in any way connect" (NB-N, 1). Stein began this long study in the austere, reductive style of the early portraits. But as she was exploring the contrasts between these two "qualities of intellect," her style began to change drastically. The more critically she distanced herself from the analytical stance that Leo represented, the more attracted she was to its polar opposite. By the end of the text, she had abandoned her previous "passion for simplification" in favor of what William James describes in "Reflex Action and Theism" as the "rival claims" of a "passion for distinguishing," which, in his words, "prefers any amount of incoherence, abruptness, and fragmentariness (so long as the literal details of the separate facts are saved)" to an abstract way of conceiving things that, while it simplifies them, dissolves away their concrete fulness" (*Essays*, p. 66).

*Tender Buttons* (1912) was the culmination of this gradual process of redefining both the "real order" of the world and the artistic order of the text that models it. The works that span this period of transition between *The Making of Americans* and *Tender Buttons* contain a succession of different styles that trace this gradual epistemological break. While writing *Two*, Stein began to experiment with new ways of using language to model a "reality" unmediated by analytical thought. At the same time, she was still working on *A Long Gay Book* and two other projects she had begun after finishing *The Making of Americans*: *G.M.P.* and *Jenny, Helen, Hannah, Paul and Peter*. She began all of these texts in the early portrait style, and *Two* was the first that she finished. Continuing to work on the others, she completed the break with her earlier methods of representation and created a concrete, radically disjunctive style to celebrate her new delight in pure difference. *Two* is by far the most interesting of these texts, because it is the only one to present clear thematic motivation for the sequence of different styles that all of them contain.

In the portraits of artists and the notebook analyses that preceded them, Stein had begun to explore the temperamental qualities that lead to successful creative activity. She continued to develop the themes as well as the techniques of these early portraits in *Two*. As in the portraits of artists, the patterning of the prose creates iconic models of the author's conception of the subjects' personalities. But the other early portraits are short texts; these techniques, sustained for more than a hundred pages, severely strain the limits of the reader's endurance of boredom. Probably this is the reason Stein's critics have had little to say about *Two*, despite its alluring subtitle.[9] Still, this far-from-"pleasurable" text rewards the reader's pain with some stretches of brilliantly innovative prose. And it is crucially important for understanding the aesthetic and epistemological issues that motivated the extreme changes in Stein's style between *The Making of Americans* and *Tender Buttons*.

The act of expression is central to her presentation of the two contrasting characters in this text: "Sound is coming out of them"; they are "expressing something." These endlessly repeated motifs dominate the first hundred pages of this long study in the portrait style. "Sound coming out of her comes out of her and is expressing sound coming out of her"—no more than that, except that "the sound coming out of her was the sound that was that she was one" (T, 9, 15). This "sound" reveals the temperament of the speakers, not by communicating specific messages but by portraying the process by which they transform their experiences into expression. As in the portrait of Nadelman and in the characterization of David Hersland, the polarities of "thinking" and "feeling" are essential to Stein's portrayal of this process in *Two*. These motifs establish the fundamental contrast between the two characters, who are never named in the text. For the woman, "feeling is everything" (23). Representing the opposite extreme, the man "was expressing that if he had not been the one thinking sound sounding would not have been coming out of him. . . . [H]e was expressing that, thinking being existing, he was existing in being thinking" (50). As this long portrait goes on, a number of related motifs come to be associated with the man's exclusive reliance on rational mediation of experience: ordering, considering, deciding, convincing, concluding, judging, reasoning, understanding, and, especially, explaining and arranging. In contrast, the woman is presented in terms of receiving, accepting, doing, working, living, and loving.

*Two* consistently patterns its language to emphasize that the man's excess of rational control is a barrier that totally insulates him from direct experience: "he *judging* that something *was angering* him *was deciding* that he *feeling* that thing he *would be* one *deciding* that he *would* not *justify* that thing the thing he *was judging*" (43–44; my emphases). This sentence surrounds "angering" and "feeling" with verbs signifying intellectual mediation and subtly manipulates their tenses, to model the habitual process described elsewhere as "arranging what he had been feeling" (46). This constant rationalization prevents the man not only from feeling but also from doing anything:

> the sound coming out of him and sounding was expressing that in reasoning he was concluding and in concluding he had expressed the reason of his understanding that someone doing something was one having done that thing, . . . that thing that he would have done if he had done that thing. (36)

Again, Stein's characteristic syntactical maneuvers marshal her limited lexicon to convey acute psychological insights. In this passage the gerundial phrase "someone doing something" is submerged in a flood of "thinking" verbs. The first part moves backward in time from "*was* expressing" to "in concluding he *had* expressed the reason of his understanding." The object of these cogitations, "someone doing something," is no sooner expressed than it is transformed into the past and, finally, into the conditional past tense of fantasy ("having done . . . would have done if he had done"). In contrast to the male character, always "intending to be expecting to be doing what he could be doing," the woman is presented as simply "doing what she was doing" (56).

The following passage models the abrupt, jerky rhythms of the man's "sound," which manifest the discontinuity between his experience and his responses:

> Coming and not coming, enjoying and being charming, jerking and not jerking, gently and with enthusiasm, brutally and not completing, occasionally and continuing, steadily and explaining, excitedly and not deciding, deciding and beginning again, completing and repeating, repeating and denying, hesitating and terrifying, angrily and beginning, angrily and completing, concluding and denying, completing and undetermined, ending without beginning, continuing with realising, ending without experiencing, . . . sound is coming out of him. (7–8)

In contrast, the woman is frequently portrayed in polysyndetic sentences that model the simple continuity of her experience and her expression:

> She being that one she was expressing and expressing she was expressing this thing and expressing this thing she was feeling everything and feeling everything she was loving and loving she was being living and being living she was continuing and being continuing sound was coming out of her and the sound coming out of her was sounding and the sound coming out of her and sounding was telling and asking anything and telling and asking anything it was expressing that she being that one was one. (47–48)

Here and elsewhere in the text, Stein uses the *gradatio*, a classical figure of thought that conventionally signals a chain of logical and chronological causality, to reinforce the continuity of the various actions she associates with her characters while obscuring the actual logic or chronology—if any—of their relationship. Throughout *Two* Stein systematically used this and other syntactical constructions to create a sense of unity and continuity that defies conventional understanding.

In contrast to the fluid continuity that is both thematized and modeled in the prose that describes the woman, a number of passages portray the disruption of simple "continuing" that the man's need for intellectual mastery entails:

> To continue, to commence to continue, to believe in continuing, to end continuing, to mean continuing, to expect continuing, to continue again, to explain continuing, to enlarge continuing, to restrict continuing, to deny continuing, to begin continuing is to arrange what can be arranged in arranging anything. (59)

Like the elder David Hersland in *The Making of Americans*, the man is constantly "beginning" ("Why does he always begin?"), while the woman's endeavors are described as both "continuing" and "beginning again and again" (76). The particular opposition that Stein intended to convey by means of these two motifs of "beginning" is far from clear in the text. In *The Making of Americans* she wrote, "It is hard to tell it about them because the same words can describe all of them the one and the other kind of them" (178). In *Two* her limited lexicon generally produces the contrasts she intended, but in this case it is necessary to resort to her notebooks for clarification:

> logical processes not reinforced by experience [are] short and never sustained. . . . Sometimes it is very good if well started, it can never run long. It is impossible that it should, it either becomes sentimentality, logic chopping, idedistic conceptions, mania or it don't go on long. Real thinking is conceptions aiming and aiming again and again always getting fuller, that is the difference between creative thinking and theorising. (NB-N, 1)

This is the model of "creative thinking" that informs *The Making of Americans*, in which the author's "beginning again and again" is a process of repetition and accumulation. In *Two* the male character resists and tries to avoid repetition, while the structures of the prose insist on the reiterated pattern that characterizes all his new beginnings:

> Sound is coming out of him, he is not allowing any piece of that thing of sound coming out of him to be coming out of him again. He is not allowing that thing. He is stating that thing quite stating that thing. Pieces of sound coming again and again out of him are pieces that he has been changing, quite changing. (7)

Although repeating is "not interesting" to him, still, "[h]e was one and sound coming out of him was sounding and repeating coming out of him was repeating that in developing he could not be repeating" (54). Even this aversion is ironically subsumed under the cycles of repetition that define his character. A defect in this "listening" accounts for his refusal to accept the inevitability of repetition: "not being listening he was not hearing that repeating should be existing" (72).

Instead of resisting and attempting to reorder the natural flow of experience, the woman is described as "resonating" in harmony with it (11). From the beginning, the text emphasizes the "complete connection" between her experience and her expression:

> Feeling that sound sounding was coming out of her she was feeling that there was complete connection between sound sounding and sound coming out of her. She was feeling that there was complete connection between sound sounding and coming out of her and something being existing. (18)

*Two* begins with a simple opposition between the man's exclusive dedication to "thinking" and the woman's sole reliance on "feeling." But gradually the woman comes to represent an ideal synthesis of these two extremes:

> *She being one she is feeling. She being one and feeling is understanding. She being one and feeling and understanding is extremely thinking.* She being one and feeling and understanding and extremely thinking is being one who is some one.
>
> In listening and in listening sound coming out and sound-

ing can be coming, in listening sound coming out of her and sounding was feeling in thinking being existing.

In listening sound coming out of her and sounding was feeling understanding being existing. In listening sound coming out of her and sounding was feeling in agreeing to have thinking be continuing. In listening sound coming out of her and sounding was *feeling that understanding is creating.* (53–54; my emphases)

In the first paragraph of this passage, one motif of action after another is introduced as a predicate and then moved to a nominative position in the next sentence. This syntactical patterning gradually forges a union of "feeling," "thinking," and "understanding," and, finally, "creating."

The woman's "complete connection" becomes the ideal of creativity modeled in the language of the text, as its ever-longer sentences use the logical order of syntax to create associations that transcend its limitations:

She would not have a decision and deciding that she would not be saying, she would be having a decision in meaning that reflection is interpretation and interpretation is decision and decision is regarding meaning and regarding meaning is acting and acting is expression and expression is not resisting winning and not resisting winning is submitting and submitting is leading and leading is declaration and declaration is beginning and beginning is intending and intending is deciding and deciding is creating and creating is not contending and not contending is destroying and destroying is submitting and submitting is decision and decision is creating and creating is leading and leading is reflection and reflection is exacting and exacting is decision and decision is meaning and meaning is progressing and progressing is not denying and not denying is feeling and feeling is thinking and thinking is arranging and arranging is continuing and continuing is rebeginning and rebeginning is submitting and submitting is deciding and deciding is creating and creating is reflecting and reflecting is meaning and meaning is deciding and deciding is believing and believing is continuing and continuing is leading and leading is expressing and expressing is meaning and meaning is feeling and feeling is submitting and submitting is deciding and deciding is creating and creating is following and following is leading and leading is following and following is deciding and deciding is creating and creating is submitting and submitting is meaning and meaning is expressing and expressing is accepting and accepting is submitting and submitting is following and following is feeling and feeling is meaning and meaning is creating and creating is doing and doing is continuing and continuing is expressing and expressing is leading and leading is following and following is expressing and expressing is meaning and meaning is expressing and expressing is leading and leading is expressing and expressing is following and following is creating and creating is expressing and expressing is meaning and meaning is doing and doing is following and following is creating and creating is leading and leading is expressing and expressing is meaning and meaning is expressing and expressing is feeling and feeling is following and feeling is leading and expressing is meaning and meaning is creating and creating is meaning and meaning is meaning. (90–91)

I quote this gargantuan sentence in its entirety to illustrate the powerfully hypnotic effect of this incantatory style. Repetition of the syntactical pattern "*A* is *B* and *B* is *C* and *C* is *D*" generates a chain of identities that eventually merges all of these motifs into an all-encompassing union. Earlier in the text these motifs were used to establish oppositions between two mutually exclusive ways of responding to experience, but the dynamic combinative process thematized and enacted in this passage embraces them all. Its cycle of identities culminates with the propositions, "expressing is meaning and meaning is creating and creating is meaning and meaning is meaning." The insistent affirmation that concludes this passage clearly reveals that Stein intended this new creative synthesis to produce an enrichment of "meaning" in her prose and not a denial of it. This point is worth emphasizing, because the passage in its entirety clearly reveals how radically she was beginning to subvert conventional logic in her pursuit of new meanings that transcend the limitations of rationality.

The elevation of the woman's "complete connection" between experience and expression into a new creative ideal was apparently not Stein's intention when she began writing *Two*. As I mentioned earlier, her notebook analyses clearly reveal that she regarded Sally and Leo Stein, the original models for this double portrait, as equally lacking the ideal balance of qualities that nurtures creativity. Her notebooks characterize Sally as a "mediumistic sensibility," extremely receptive to experience but lacking the intellectual power to produce original work (NB-N, 1).[10] The early pages of *Two* attribute to the female character some of the negative traits Stein described in her notebook analysis of her sister-in-law: "not being then a strong one" (19); "suffering" (21); and extreme passivity (43). But as the passages quoted above illustrate, this character, with her "complete connection" between experience and expression, gradually came to represent Stein's own creative ideal as she continued to work on the text. But perhaps this was not quite as much of a deviation from her original plan as I have been suggesting. Although the title page of the manuscript identifies its subjects as "Leo and Sally," the notes she wrote on the text consistently refer to the man as Leo and to the woman as "Jane."[11] She assigned the name "Jane Sands" to Sally Stein in *A Long Gay Book* (NB, fragment #14). But in her notebooks she also sometimes used "Jane Sands" or "Jane Sandys" as pseudonyms for herself (NB-10, 6). Whatever her initial intentions, the text itself reveals the gradual process of reevaluation that eventually resulted in the idealization of this character.

While she departed so far from her original analysis of Sally's shortcomings, she never deviated from her focus on Leo's weaknesses. In fact, her relentless probing of the limitations of her brother's exclusive commitment to rationality seems to have impelled her to define her own creativity in radical opposition to the intellectual stance he represented. Although she cast it in the form of an anonymous study of contrasting personalities, *Two* was by far the most personal work Stein had written since *Q.E.D.* Her first intellectual model, her brother Leo had played a major role in shaping her ideas and tastes. He led her to Harvard and into William James's classes. A few years later she followed him to Europe and into the center of the creative ferment of avant-garde painting. In 1908 they shared the excitement of reading Weininger's *Sex and Character*.[12] During their early years in Paris, Leo's talk dominated their salon. He considered himself an artist, an aesthetician, and a philosopher. He proved incapable of sustained efforts in any of these fields, although he seems to have talked brilliantly about them all. Stein's notebooks reveal that Leo continued to be an important source of aesthetic insights and intellectual stimulation for her as late as 1909.[13] Soon after that, their relationship became strained close to the breaking point. Leo never recognized the value of his sister's work. He scorned it as absolutely, and perhaps as jealously, as he did Picasso's cubist paintings. In 1913 he described "cubism whether in paint or ink" as "tommyrot," the "intellectual product of the unintellectual."[14] Meanwhile, Stein had found in Picasso a continuing source of stimulation for her own work and in Alice B. Toklas a new source of emotional support. Although her final break with Leo did not occur until the fall of 1913, when he moved out of the rue de Fleurus apartment, her psychological separation was apparently completed in the process of writing *Two*.[15]

Significantly, the character Stein created to represent an idealized alternative to Leo's tyrannical rationality was a woman. This in itself signals a striking change in Stein's conception of her role as an artist and as a woman.[16] Beginning with Leo, all of her artistic and intellectual models had been male—James, Weininger, Cézanne, Matisse, and Picasso. A woman who was a serious artist in the first decade of this century was even more of an anomaly in France than in America or England. In Stein's circle in Paris, Apollinaire's mistress Marie Laurencin and Sonia Delaunay, the wife of Robert Delaunay, were the only female artists. Stein's *Autobiography of Alice B. Toklas* accurately reflects the attitude of that time by presenting these women primarily as appendages of the male artists and only incidentally as painters in their own right.

Stein herself, a woman artist who was also a lesbian, initially responded to the multiple social paradoxes of her identity by defining herself completely in terms of male models. In *Q.E.D.*, the most transparently autobiographical of all her works, her heroine paradoxically remarks, "I always did thank God I wasn't born a woman" (58). In this early text, each of the women involved in the romantic triangle is referred to at least once as a "man" (71, 80, 109). Stein easily transformed Adele into Jeff Campbell in "Melanctha." A few years later, she created David Hersland to portray a version of her own development. The invidious sexual stereotypes in Weininger's *Sex and Character* only reinforced this tendency to define herself entirely in masculine terms: "Picasso has a maleness that belongs to genius. Moi ausi, perhaps" (NB-C, 21). In this context, *Two*'s opposition between the sterile rationality of the male and the fluid creativity of the female in itself suggests a major change in Stein's conception of her role as an artist. While she was working on *Two*, she also wrote "Orta or One Dancing," her portrait of Isadora Duncan. The first text in this series to portray a woman artist, it attributes to its character the same creative fusion of "feeling," "thinking," "believing," "expressing," and "meaning" that characterizes the woman in *Two*.[17]

After she had completed more than one hundred pages of *Two*, Stein wrote a passage that reads as a virtual apotheosis of female creativity:

> [S]he is the one having a connection that expressing is the thing that rising again has risen, and rising is rising and will be having come to be risen. She is the anticipation of forfeiting what is not forbidden. She is the anticipation of conviction of remembering being existing. She is the anticipating of a new one having been an old one. She is the anticipation of expression having immaculate conception. She is the anticipation of crossing. She is the anticipation of regeneration. She is the anticipation of excelling obligation. She is the anticipation. She is the actualisation. She is the rising having been arisen. She is the convocation of anticipation and acceptation. She is the lamb and the lion. She is the leaven of reverberation. She is the complication of receiving, she is the articulation of forgetting, she is the expression of indication, she is the augmentation of condensing, she is the inroad of releasing. (107-8)

This exalted language incorporates both the rhythms and the traditional symbols of incantatory religious prose.[18] Its richly evocative imagery breaks the stylistic constraints Stein had rigorously enforced in her prose for a number of years.

In the early part of *Two*, even as Stein was thematizing the limitations of the male character's conceptual ordering of experience, her own methods of rendering character were still grounded in the same reductive theory of personality that governed her previous work. Her techniques of abstracting motifs of repeated actions and carefully arranging them to model her conception of the static essence of personality were closer to the male character's habits of filtering and "arranging" experience than to the female's "complete connection" between experience and expression.

But the "inroad of releasing" that is powerfully thematized and enacted in the passage quoted above was far from the first manifestation of Stein's desire to liberate her writing from what she had come to regard as the restrictive bonds of rational control. As I have already emphasized, many earlier passages in *Two*, like this one, repeat a particular syntactical pattern to create a web of interconnections that defy conventional logic. What distinguishes the passage quoted above from previous ones is its greater freedom of lexical choices. The narrow range of established motifs of repeated actions gives way to a far broader, freer range of associations. But even in this one the associative flow is still channeled, into the area of traditional religious imagery. Transcending conventional logical order, its patterned language creates a richly reverberating field of signification.

Stein seems to have used this technique of syntactical repetition for a time as a device for freeing her associations from the order of rationality. While she was writing this section of *Two*, she was also experimenting with another way of using repetition to release the flow of her language. In a number of paragraphs shortly after the "inroad of releasing" passage, repetition of sound generates a chain of associations:

> He who not lightly when he lightly and shining brightly
> was saying that the sun if he won, that the sun having being the

sun and he seeing the sun then he seeing the sun and the sun
being, then he won. He was the one and he was the one who
did not win and this he said as he said he won and he won. He
did win. (110)

In *Jenny, Helen, Hannah, Paul and Peter* Stein wrote, "The only
way to forget is to go on repeating" (220). But in fact, toward the
end of *Two* and in the other texts she was writing at the same time,
she eventually abandoned this use of repetition. Apparently she no
longer needed this mechanical device for overriding the strictures of
rational control.

After B. F. Skinner's 1934 essay "Has Gertrude Stein a Secret?" claimed that the "secret" of her *Tender Buttons* style was her
use of automatic writing, Stein took pains to counter Skinner's al-
legation. She insisted that her Harvard experiments, which were
central to Skinner's argument, had convinced her "there is no such
thing as automatic writing" (EA, 264).[19] At that time Stein was apparently eager to dissociate her own aesthetic premises from those
of the surrealists. Beginning with Breton's first manifesto in 1924,
automatism was at the center of the surrealist program for liber-
ating the unconscious:

> SURREALISM, n.    Pure psychic automatism by which it is pro-
> posed to express, either orally, or in writing, or in any other
> manner, the real functioning of thought. Dictation of thought,
> in the absence of all control exercised by reason, beyond all
> aesthetic or moral preoccupations.[20]

Stein always professed a lack of interest in surrealism.[21] Some of the
texts the surrealists produced strikingly resemble Stein's writings in
the *Tender Buttons* style. But the Freudian model of the unconscious that was central to their theoretical premises was foreign
to her own conception of human consciousness. In the texts that
immediately preceded *Tender Buttons*, however, the word "automatic" appears a number of times, in contexts that suggest that
Stein was indeed thinking of her writing as a modified form of
automatism at that time: "The movement is not so automatic that
there will be any disuse" (GMP, 248). In *Two*, she used the tech-

niques I have described to generate associations that violated logical order, but she never entirely relinquished control of her thematic focus. And "aesthetic preoccupations," which Breton somewhat naïvely proposed to leave behind in surrealist writing, were prominent in Stein's deliberate experiments in liberation. As another text she wrote at this time directly states, "Automatic action is creation, creation is a mingling of more" (JHHPP, 234).

"A mingling of more" is an apt description of the series of stylistic transformations that began to appear near the end of *Two* and in the other texts she was working on in 1912. A manuscript note for *Jenny, Helen, Hannah, Paul and Peter* signals the first change: "Make it dramatic. Not characters, relations" (NB, fragment #162). In the early pages of both this text and *G.M.P.*, Stein abandoned her habitual method of repeating motifs of internal actions to portray essential character. Instead, she used verbs of activity to create choreographic studies of group interactions. Stein originally conceived of *G.M.P.* as a study in relationships between the group of painters and admirers surrounding Matisse and those around Picasso, a subject she first treated in the early portrait of Matisse. Unlike the portraits, *G.M.P.* is not concerned with either the aesthetics or the personalities of the two painters; it is purely a study of physical movements. The central motifs of its opening pages are "coming," "going," and "staying," interspersed with "talking," "listening," and "sitting"—the physical actions of social intercourse without any of its content. But repetition, the primary characteristic of Stein's style beginning with *Three Lives*, soon disappears in these texts and in *Two* as well, ceding to a new mode of discontinuous narrative. A wider variety of simple past-tense verbs of activity replaces the repeated motifs that presented all actions as continuing states in her earlier texts. Sequences of shorter sentences present discrete actions that have no apparent logical or chronological relationship to one another. No longer unified by repetition, the paragraph becomes a purely formal, rhythmical structure.

Before she finished writing *Two*, Stein was formulating a new sense of an all-inclusive "reality" in these terms:

> What the way the union of all that is everything comes to
> have with all that is everything is the way of explaining every-
> thing, is the way of saying everything. . . . There is all there.
> There is the rest of any whole. There is enough and too much is
> not enough, enough is more than any piece and all is enough.
> (T, 119)

In *Two* this sense of "the union of all that is everything" took the
form of logically disjunctive series of "pieces" of past-tense actions.
In some passages these actions are rendered in concrete detail:

> A distant noise was farther than he heard and this was be-
> cause he had defective hearing. He was alight and this was
> showing when he stood where he stood and his clothes were
> burning. . . . He removed the pieces of wood that were ham-
> mered on several large boxes and the way he worked was very
> strong. He sandpapered a table and lifted heavy weights. He
> arranged a simple machine. (107)

More frequently, the text presents transitive actions without specific objects, denuded of causes or effects. The following passage
illustrates the kind of specific but context-free actions that pervade
this new mode of narrative:

> On the return of the meeting he was not coming to be re-
> engaging all the pleasant terms of dancing. He did not show
> that every night was coming. He had the safe union of the
> meeting that is not assuaging staying. He did not lose every-
> thing. He said it all then. He stayed in the room where no evi-
> dence was accumulating. He was the arbiter then. He saw the
> rest. He said it. He was not interested in all that there was to
> hear. He did listen. He would not deny anything. He was not
> younger than all the same. He was not younger and older. He
> did it with pleasant intention. He was not all the same. He was
> not younger. He gave what there was when he gave what there
> was. He determined then. He judged the rest as he wrote what
> he wrote. He was not life-like when he changed all the conse-
> quences. He did the same. He changed then. (113–14)

In this discontinuous narrative, all actions have an equal value. None is more significant than any of the others. In *The Making of Americans* Stein's desire for "completed understanding" took the form of totalizing conceptions that obliterated all individual differences. In *Two* and the texts that followed, she rejected all such methods of "reducing that which is confusing to that which is so clear" and expressed her sense of "union" in the opposite form, by creating inventories of diverse particulars (119). In her own words,

> To accept that interest is to use that time and to use that time is to take a piece of any day and say the time there is to say what is said. Sound sounding is expressing everything.
>
> If the movement is all day then there is all of any day and that interest is that expression. There can be no remainder. There is no alloy. There is that sound. There is that day. There is every day. There is sound sounding. There is all of that. There is that. (136–37)

Toward the end of *Two*, Stein was already considering a new method of writing, in which the act of expression is simultaneous with the "piece of any day" that is being rendered: "Correlation between the past and the connection is not the only way to achieve the present expression. The logic and the conception and the *actuality in the wagon* all that which is not prearranged is convincing" (129; my emphasis). In this work her continuing focus on the past actions of her characters largely precluded this "actuality" of concrete objects from being represented in her prose. In the other texts she went on writing after finishing *Two*, she suddenly abandoned her original subjects to focus directly on the present-tense "actuality" of a "piece of any day." In *G.M.P.*, *A Long Gay Book*, and *Jenny, Helen, Hannah, Paul and Peter*, the style changes suddenly and radically. Concrete nouns and adjectives inventory the heterogeneous richness of present-tense perception, and syntax joins them together in startling new combinations that defy our ordinary conception of "reality."

Stein began to create this new style in the summer of 1912, while she was vacationing in Spain with Alice B. Toklas.[22] Her happiness seems to have overflowed into the pages of *G.M.P.*:

> There is more enjoyment than there is laughing. There is more laughing than there is decision. All the rest comes some way.
>
> To be there where morning mingles with something is the same time as most pleasure. (248)

Descriptions are grounded in spatial and temporal immediacy: "It was not strange that the cow came out and the square was there and the heat was strong. It was not strange yesterday" (249). In straightforward language, the text records a momentous event: "One bed was used. This was a change" (248). Shortly after this, somewhat more allusive prose celebrates sexual consummation: "The pleasure is not the same and the reason is more. There is that pleasure in all union. The hands are there and so are the feet and all in between and above are complete" (250). The words "wedding," "marriage," and "union" recur throughout the second half of *G.M.P.* The joy of erotic union expands to encompass the most ordinary details of daily life: "So much wedding, so much distribution, so many night shirt-waists and so many linen dusters accepted, so much breakfast and nothing sooner, such a joy is without alloy" (253). "A long simple bath is contiguous to a certainty" (250). Food, clothing, household goods, horses—all these contiguous objects take part in this celebration of sensuality.

As she began reveling in the heterogeneous plenitude of this new "reality," Stein's new "passion for distinguishing" led her to dismiss the most fundamental premises of her previous "passion for simplification": "There was no repetition" (260). In the intensity of this sensuous immediacy, "[t]here is no sense so simple that it is resembling" (262). I reintroduce the terminology of William James's essay "The Sentiment of Rationality" at this point to emphasize that the new style Stein began to create in 1912 was not a flight from "reality" but an artistic model of what James described in this essay as the only "real order of the world": "*The real world as it is given objectively at this moment is the sum total of all its beings and events now. . . . [C]ollateral contemporaneity, and nothing else, is the real order of the world*" (*Essays*, pp. 118–19). This formulation accurately describes the alternative idea of "reality" that informed Stein's new style. Her fundamental goal of using language to model a "direct relationship to the object" remained unchanged. But in the process of writing *Two* she radically redefined both her object of representation and her epistemological model. Stein's manuscript notes indicate that when this new style first appeared in *G.M.P.*, she planned to return to her human subjects.[23] But the new "music of the present tense" lured her away from this project (GMP, 252). In *G.M.P.* she soon redefined her subject as "creation." In all of the texts she was writing at that time, she went on exploring the expressive possibilities and theoretical implications of this concrete, logically disjunctive style. After she returned to Paris in the autumn of 1912, she wrote *Tender Buttons*, her most brilliant model of the "concrete chaos" that James described as the "real order" of a "piece of any day."[24]

*Tender Buttons*:
"The Music of the Present Tense"

N *Tender Buttons* Stein channeled the flood of concrete particulars she first tapped in *G.M.P.* to create an artfully structured composition. Its three sections, "Objects," "Food," and "Rooms," form a provocative sequence. From the external objects we see and touch, the text moves inward to the substances we ingest and, in the final section, outward again to the spaces that surround us. *Tender Buttons* describes a female world (circa 1912) of domestic objects and rituals—a world of dresses and hats, tables and curtains, mealtimes and bedtimes, cleanliness and dirt. Although a few exotic items, including an elephant and a "white hunter," make momentary appearances, the iconography of domestic life dominates the text. Concrete nouns and adjectives name a wealth of homely particulars. But in its artful rearrangement of these details, the text models a world in which objects, foods, and rooms are liberated from their normal subordination to human routines and purposes.

Stripped of this customary order, buttons can be "tender." We know that steaks and hearts can be tender. But buttons? Our everyday assumptions tell us that the phrase "tender buttons" is nonsense. Normally, our prior knowledge of the function of objects lets us perceive things as unobtrusive instruments of human ends. Without this knowledge of its mundane function, a plush button could appear quite tender; a young child could easily assume it was edible. Beginning with Cézanne's and Picasso's still lifes, modernist artists have revealed the strangeness of familiar objects, seen as if for the first time. Duchamp's famous exhibition of the urinal inaugurated a new fascination with "found objects," removed from their normal contexts and habituating functions. Merle Oppenheim's fur cup and, more recently, Oldenburg's fans and other "soft" re-creations of manufactured objects transgress the order of everyday experience more violently, by transforming these domestic objects into bizarre artifacts that totally violate the functionality of cups and fans.

Stein's "tender buttons" lack the obstinate concreteness of these physical objects; they cannot be seen or touched. But concrete nouns and adjectives call things to mind, and syntax can bind them together in startling new combinations. The particular pleasure that *Tender Buttons* provides is this kind of artful reordering of the familiar world. Because it systematically refuses to "make sense" in any conventional way, many of its readers, admirers and detractors alike, have assumed too readily that Stein had begun to use words as "unencumbered plastic entities" (Brinnin), "removed from their intellectual, semantic straitjackets" (Weinstein).[1] But the power of language to name concrete things is crucially important in *Tender Buttons*, as Stein herself insisted in "Poetry and Grammar":

> And then, something happened and I began to discover the names of things, that is not discover the names but discover the things the things to see the things to look at and in so doing I had of course to name them not to give them new names but to see that I could find out how to know that they were there by their names or by replacing their names. And how was I to do so? They had their names and naturally I called them by the names they had and in doing so having begun looking at them I called them by their names with passion and that made poetry, I did not mean it to make poetry but it did, it made the *Tender Buttons*. (LIA, 235)

In "Portraits and Repetition," Stein explains that she began writing these "portraits of things and enclosures . . . of rooms and food and everything" because she "needed to completely face the difficulty of how to include what is seen." She explicitly compares this new orientation with the aesthetic concerns of painters: "they had too to be certain that looking was not confusing itself with remembering" (LIA, 188–89). She suggests that painters turn to still lifes for the same reason she began writing "portraits of things," because human subjects inevitably invite "remembering" and "recognizing resemblances." In 1912 the Steins' collection of paintings

included Cézanne's *Apples* (1873–77) and a number of Cézannesque still lifes Picasso painted in 1908 and 1909.[2] Cézanne's still
lifes revolutionized that genre in painting, and Stein's "portraits of
things" were written in the spirit of the break with the tradition that
his paintings instigated. In a brilliant discussion of Cézanne's treatment of objects, Meyer Schapiro argues that, although this genre is
defined by the absence of human subjects, before Cézanne it was
used to express "our being as masters of nature, as artisans and tool
users. Its development coincides with the growth of landscape;
both belong to the common process of the humanizing of culture
through the discovery of nature's all-inclusiveness and man's power of transforming his environment." In contrast, the arrangements
of objects in Cézanne's paintings "have nothing of the formality of
a human purpose. . . . The world of proximate things, like the distant landscape, exists for Cézanne as something to be contemplated
rather than used, and it exists in a kind of pre-human, natural disorder which has first to be mastered by the artist's method of construction."[3]

   In his still lifes of 1909, Picasso was working with Cézannesque arrangements of fruit and glassware on tables, rendering
these forms to suggest three-dimensional space and at the same
time to participate in the overall geometrical patterning of the surface design. By 1910 he had broken the closed form. Interlocking
monochromatic planes which do not correspond to the contours of
objects cover the entire surface of his "analytical" cubist paintings,
and objects are notated by synecdochic signs, fragmentary parts of
their outlines. Beginning in 1911 the iconography of "analytical"
cubism began to include printed words as well as these fragmentary
iconic signs.[4] In Picasso's *Architect's Table* (1912), one of the
paintings in Stein's collection, the words "Marc" (alluding to the
bottles of Vieux Marc Picasso had previously painted) and "La
Jolie" appear, along with a painted facsimile of Gertrude Stein's
calling card. Fragmentary outlines notate upholstery fringe and the
scrolled shape of the arm of a chair. These signs seem to float freely
on a linear grid of intersecting rectangular planes. Unlike Picasso's
still lifes of 1908 and 1909, these paintings no longer present iconic
models of the spatial order of visual perceptions. The synecdochic

iconic signs still retain a degree of direct resemblance to the familiar objects they signify, but in the external world, musical instruments, glasses, bottles, newspapers, and pipes would never appear in the spatial configurations these canvases create.

In May 1912, shortly before Stein left for Spain, Picasso created the first cubist collage, *Still-life with Chair Caning*.[5] The bottom of the picture is dominated by a piece of oilcloth with a printed pattern of chair caning, and the oval canvas is surrounded by a piece of rope. Soon both Picasso and Braque began including fragments of newspaper, wallpaper, cigarette wrappers, tickets, sand, cloth, and even cut-out pictures of objects in their compositions. These paradoxical signs are absolutely "real," literal pieces of the objects they signify, but they are starkly juxtaposed to one another in an order that bears no resemblance to that of the everyday world they came from.

Within months after Picasso created his first collage, Stein invented the newly concrete, logically disjunctive style that culminated in *Tender Buttons*. The process of epistemological questioning that led Stein to this radical stylistic reversal occurred during the same short period of time in which Picasso had also been radically changing his methods of representation, in remarkably similar ways. Shortly after Picasso abandoned closed forms and, with them, the effort to depict volumes as the essential characteristic of objects, Stein rejected her previous efforts to model the static essence of personalities. Picasso developed new signs for objects that traced fragments of their outlines; Stein began to represent specific, random actions, "pieces of any day." And, in 1912, each created a new method of representation, using signs that were far more "concrete" than the austere, allusive iconography of their previous compositions. Stein was not merely imitating Picasso's most recent work; her texts clearly reveal the internal logic of her stylistic reversal. Still, these analogous movements from unity and closure to fragmentation and disjunction strongly suggest that Picasso's work was a continuing stimulus for Stein's reevaluation of her own methods of representation.

And the parallels between Stein's work and Picasso's can be characterized even more precisely than this. Roman Jakobson's

seminal essay "Two Aspects of Language and Two Types of Aphasic Disturbances" uses the speech of aphasiacs to chart the two
poles of discourse he labels the metaphoric and the metonymic.[6] In
Jakobson's terms, between 1910 and 1912 the semiotic structures
of Picasso's paintings and Stein's writings both changed in analogous ways—from the limits of the metonymic pole to the opposite
extreme. In *The Making of Americans* and the early portraits,
Stein's discourse strikingly resembles the model of aphasic speech
Jakobson uses to exemplify the metonymic pole of discourse. This
extreme is characterized by an avoidance of naming. Specific nouns
are replaced by general ones. Key words are dropped or replaced by
abstract substitutes. "Words with an inherent reference to context,
like pronouns and pronominal adverbs, and words serving merely
to construct the context, such as connectives and auxiliaries are
particularly prone to survive. . . . *Only the framework, the connecting links of communication, is spared.*"[7] In *The Making of
Americans* and the early portraits, Stein's style systematically foregrounds these "connecting links of discourse" and avoids specific
names of persons or things. The few nouns that appear are as general as they can be ("something," "anything," "a thing"), and pronouns systematically substitute for proper names. Subordinating
conjunctions and relative pronouns are crucial elements of this
style, and auxiliary verbs proliferate.

Picasso's "analytical" cubist paintings of 1910 and 1911 are
characterized by a similar paucity of iconic signs. Like the texts
Stein wrote during the same years, these compositions are dominated by connective signs—the increasingly complex networks of
intersecting planes, painted with closely hatched brushstrokes. In
*Cubism and Twentieth-Century Art* Robert Rosenblum uses linguistic terms to describe the restricted iconography and syntactical
complexity of these compositions: "On the one hand, the vocabulary, in its almost complete restriction to flattened arcs and straight
lines and its abstention from irrelevant literal detail, has reached
a pristine simplicity. On the other hand, the syntax has achieved an
infinite sophistication revealed, for example, in the endlessly intricate shifting of planes within a hairbreadth, or in the equally rich
variations of light and dark that make this gossamer scaffolding

quiver in unpredictable ways upon the white surface of the paper."[8]

Cubist collage reverses these structural polarities. The intricate patterns of intersecting planes that form the compositional scaffolding of "analytical" cubist paintings disappear. Synecdochic iconic signs, including literal pieces of "real" objects, are simply juxtaposed to one another or overlaid, one overlapping the next. This stark "asyntactical" arrangement of iconic signs on a rigorously flat plane is analogous to what Jakobson terms the metaphoric pole of discourse, in which speech consists of nothing but names. Conjunctions, prepositions, pronouns, auxiliaries—all the connective signs of discourse disappear. Instead of well-formed sentences, there are only "word-heaps."[9] In the new style Stein began to create in the summer of 1912, concrete nouns and adjectives are abundant. Occasionally an agrammatical "word-heap" like "Black ink best wheel bale brown" appears in *Tender Buttons* (476). Although this kind of asyntactical succession of words is rare, it delimits this style as the antithesis of the syntactical complexity of Stein's previous texts. The pronouns, subordinating conjunctions, and auxiliary verbs that were foregrounded in *The Making of Americans* and the early portraits are absent from *Tender Buttons*. In this text, simple present-tense sentences use straightforward conventional syntax to link concrete nouns and adjectives together. The startling new arrangements that these sentences create bear as little resemblance to the habitual order of the objects they name as Picasso's collages have to the familiar contexts in which their "real" pieces of objects ordinarily appear.

Ignoring these structural changes from one polar extreme to the other, Jakobson characterizes cubism as metonymic, because the "object is transformed into a set of synecdoches."[10] This points to a fundamental problem with Jakobson's analysis. Applying his model to the constitution of individual signs and to the structural relationships among both signifiers and objects signified, he never deals with the fact that characteristics of the two polar extremes sometimes coexist, at different levels of analysis, in the same structures. In cubist collage, the individual signs are metonymic, but the syntax is close to the metaphorical pole. Not only are connective signs suppressed, but, in addition, complex visual and ver-

bal puns create relationships of equivalence, which are characteristic of metaphorical discourse. In Picasso's *Still-life with Violin
and Fruit,* for example, the curved shape cut out of newspaper in
the upper left signifies a plate. This shape is duplicated in the curved
piece of white paper in the lower center, which is bounded at its
bottom edge by another piece of newspaper. In this position, the
newspaper signifies only itself. This collage illustrates how complex Picasso's signs have become. Newspaper stands for itself,
but it is also cut to form the shape of a plate and a table edge. In
addition, the words in the newspaper headlines create some of
the multimedia puns the cubists loved so well: "La vie sportif,"
"[app]arition," and, finally, "[Jo]urnal." And the newspaper plays
still another role, as background for fragmentary sketches of a gob-
let and a violin.

This freedom to put into play such different kinds of signs is, of
course, impossible in writing. Language is a closed system of arbitrary signs; it cannot present a literal piece of an object. Nouns and
adjectives are the most "concrete" resources of language, but they
are the names of things and attributes and not the things themselves. Still, language brings things to mind by calling their names,
and sounds and syntax can create relationships among them that
are as complex and multiple as the ones in cubist collage. "A splice
is something that causes a connection," Stein wrote in *G.M.P.*
(258). Appositional structures and propositions of identity systematically assert their conventional power to "cause connections" of
equivalence among these names of objects and sensation. Repetition of words and phonemes and complex puns reinforce the pre-
vailing structural principle of similarity. But the nouns that are
linked together in this text are not semantically equivalent; their
relationship is what Jakobson describes as metonymic, not metaphoric. In a figural sense, they are all synecdoches, naming contiguous "pieces of any day."[11] In this text all the connective links
of syntax are pressed into service to "splice" concrete nouns and
adjectives together into new configurations that challenge our customary sense of the order of things.

Years later, Stein described the power of Picasso's photographs of groups of objects he had carefully arranged: "I have kept

one of [these photographs], and by the force of his vision it was not necessary that he paint the picture. To have brought the objects together already changed them to other things, not to another picture but to something else, to things as Picasso saw them" (P, 18). The characteristic method of the "still lifes" in *Tender Buttons* depends on this transformative power of juxtaposition. The following passage invites the reader to recognize this affinity between the verbal "portraits of objects" in *Tender Buttons* and the still lifes of Cézanne and Picasso:

> There was a whole collection made. A damp cloth, an oyster, a single mirror, a mannikin, a student, a silent star, a single spark, a little movement and the bed is made. This shows the disorder, it does, it shows more likeness than anything else, it shows the single mind that directs an apple. (TB, 501–2)

The objects named in this collection are simply joined together in the middle sentence, with no indication of the relationships among them. Assonance and consonance create a high degree of sound equivalence, but there is no accompanying semantic coherence in the series. A single mirror, a mannikin, and a student could inhabit the same dress shop. A student could be called a "silent star," which in turn, could be substituted for a "single spark." The two associative principles of similarity and contiguity are at work in this catalogue, but neither one predominates.

Bracketing this chaotic inventory, the first and third sentence assert the artfulness of this "collection," deliberately assembled to "show the disorder" as it "shows more likeness than anything else." This is only one of many affirmations that the principle of mimesis is still operative in *Tender Buttons*. Its deliberate disordering of the everyday world models what William James called the "concrete chaos" of immediate sensory experience, in which "collateral contemporaneity" is the only "real order." Its particular configurations of names show more about the operations of the "single mind that directs an apple" than about any objective ordering of things in the world. But as the final clause reminds us, this text is far from a literal transcription of the immediate sense-data that enter the "stream of consciousness." Like the Cézanne and

Picasso still lifes of apples that hung on the walls of Stein's atelier, it is a deliberate artistic model, not a naïve reproduction, of the "real."

From beginning to end, *Tender Buttons* is this kind of lecture-demonstration in aesthetics and epistemology. At one point, the discourse parodically calls attention to its pedagogical methods: "Lecture, lecture and repeat instructions" (483). But this didactic discourse is informed by radical skepticism: "What language can instruct any fellow" (483). The first "portrait" in "Objects" introduces the reader to the methods of the text by illustrating some of the fundamental problems of describing any object:

> A CARAFE, THAT IS A BLIND GLASS
> A kind in glass and a cousin, a spectacle and nothing strange a single hurt color and an arrangement in a system to pointing. All this and not ordinary, not unordered in not resembling. The difference is spreading. (461)

As soon as it names the carafe, the discourse introduces a "blind glass" as the first in a series of appositional substitutions that demonstrate the difficulty of describing the uniqueness of any particular object in terms of resemblance. It is a "kind" in the larger category of glassware and a "cousin" to a "glass." But so many things are made of glass. Compared to "spectacles," perhaps, this "glass" is "blind." As these words explode into multiple meanings, none of them can convey the singular quality of a particular carafe. Like most of the others portrayed in the text, it is a commonplace object, "nothing strange." But it is presented as a "spectacle" in the double sense of the word, both an exciting sight in itself and a focusing device, to create a new way of seeing. The final term completes the series by emphasizing that all of this is an "arrangement in a system" of designation ("pointing"). The second sentence thematizes the lesson that the first one demonstrates in another chain of substitutions: "All this and not ordinary, not unordered in not resembling." The structure of the discourse is totally metaphoric until the final sentence, which introduces the only verb in the piece, to emphasize that difference, not resemblance, is the epistemological order that dominates this text.

The discourse of *Tender Buttons* systematically plays with, and against, these oppositions between similarity and difference, substitution and predication, which correspond to the fundamental operations of language. But from the beginning, "difference is spreading," calling into question all conventional modes of order, including language itself, that substitute limited resemblances for the chaotic particularity of the phenomenal world. In *Tender Buttons*, "a spectacle is the resemblance between a circular side place and nothing else, nothing else" (468). In her earlier texts, Stein manipulated the material resources of language in new ways, to create iconic models that embodied her conviction that the truth of human character resided in repetition and resemblance. By the time she wrote *Tender Buttons*, she had become convinced that "[t]here is no sense so simple that it is resembling" (GMP, 262). If difference reigns supreme in the immediate sense-data of experience, then "there is no correct description" of this "reality" within the realm of language (GMP, 258). *Tender Buttons* systematically demonstrates that the inherent order of language is equally alien to the concrete heterogeneity of the external physical world and to the chaotic richness of immediate perceptual experience.

Throughout *Tender Buttons*, the words "arrangement," "system," and "order" recur, to emphasize that the text is "not unordered in not resembling" more conventional modes of writing. Repetition of these and other sets of words is one of the devices by which this text creates its own artful order that contains the chaotic particularity it both thematizes and demonstrates.[12] One complex of images asserts the fundamental principle of difference— breaking, shattering, division, pieces, remainders. Another invokes a "wholeness" that is based on the mingling of heterogeneous elements: collections, mixtures, reunions, stews. Persistent commentary on its own operations further contributes to the thematic coherence of this text. Time and again the discourse asserts the particular order that informs its "portraits of things": "A sound, a whole sound is not separation, a whole sound is in an order" (TB, 480). Although the descriptions in the first two sections have individual objects as their starting points, in *Tender Buttons* "[a] single image is not splendor. . . . A charm a single charm is doubtful"

(463, 464). The "charm" is in the combinations of concrete nouns and adjectives that mingle in each "portrait," arranged in purely artistic order by the operations of language.

"A Feather," one of the early pieces in "Objects," clearly illustrates this combinative method:

> A feather is trimmed, it is trimmed by the light and the bug and the post, it is trimmed by little leaning and by all sorts of mounted reserves and loud volumes. It is surely cohesive. (473)

This feather is "trimmed" by what surrounds it in two senses of the word, both "decorated" and "reduced to order." This is one of the few "portraits" that the reader can easily normalize by supplying a realistic context in which all of these elements appear. The feather on a hat is seen against the background of a post, a light, and a passing bug. A parade is going by, with "mounted reserves" and "loud volumes" of music. The feather, itself, is "leaning." But perhaps it is the wearer who is leaning against the post. This overinterpretation destroys the particular "charm" of the piece, which deliberately refuses to provide the kind of realistic motivation that would normalize the collection of disparate elements that "trims" the feather. Throughout the text, each individual object is portrayed as similarly "cohesive," its singularity heightened by the juxtaposition of contiguous particulars.

The concern with vision and visual description that is evident in the pieces I have been discussing continues throughout the text. Names of colors and adjectives describing the qualities of light are abundant in Stein's "portraits of things." Lines and outlines, surfaces, centers, lengths, widths, and measurements evoke the compositional resources and structures of painting. But the *chosisme* of *Tender Buttons* is as far from Robbe-Grillet's "littérature objective" of the 1950s as it is from Ponge's meditations on the meanings of concrete objects. Robbe-Grillet's early novels use the language of geometrical description to "register the distance" between the object and the self.[13] *Tender Buttons* systematically collapses this distance, as the title itself indicates. Buttons are "tender," a glass is "blind," a color is "hurt," food is "kind." An interpenetration of mind and matter animates the portrayal of concrete objects: "Enthusiastically hurting a clouded yellow bud and saucer, enthusiastically so is the bite in the ribbon" (470). Many of Stein's "still lifes" include emotional and kinetic qualities:

### A METHOD OF A CLOAK

A single climb to a line, a straight exchange to a cane, a desperate adventure and courage and a clock, all this which is a system, which has feeling, which has resignation and success, all makes an attractive black silver. (464)

"A single climb to a line" animates the description at the outset; "a desperate adventure and courage" increases the sense of drama surrounding the object. "A clock" abruptly breaks the mounting tension by introducing a suggestion of a man-made order. "All this," the discourse claims, "is a system." In all of these pieces, syntax and sound associations forge names of disparate emotions, actions, and objects into formally coherent "systems."

While its concrete objects are animated with human qualities, *Tender Buttons* presents human beings simply as physical objects, equal to all the others named and arranged in these "still lifes": "and so between curves and outlines and real seasons and more out glasses and a perfectly unprecedented arrangement between old ladies and mild colds there is no satin wood shining" (473). Here, as in "A Feather" and many other pieces, spatial contiguity is the ordering principle of this "perfectly unprecedented arrangement," but "mild colds" and "real seasons" mingle with the "curves and outlines" of purely spatial configurations. Sometimes the human body is reduced to a set of synecdoches, as in "Colored Hats": "Colored hats are necessary to show that curls are worn by an addition of blank spaces, this makes the difference between single lines and broad stomachs" (473). Occasionally the discourse creates shocking juxtapositions of human bodies and inanimate objects, as in "Little sales ladies little sales ladies little saddles of mutton" (475). This equation of "little sales ladies" with pieces of meat strikingly illustrates how radically the order of *Tender Buttons* refuses to privilege human meanings and purposes. In her earlier

works, Stein portrayed human beings in terms of essential character, abstracted from their concrete daily life in the physical world.
The radical reversal in *Tender Buttons* suggests not so much a de-
humanization as a new affirmation that human existence is intimately involved with the physicality of matter and of flesh. The
physical world portrayed in *Tender Buttons* includes the most intimate realities of the female body. "A Petticoat" shows "a disgrace,
an ink spot, a rosy charm" (471). And a "shallow hole rose on red,
a shallow hole in and in this makes ale less," an obvious transmuta-
tion of Alice (474).

At a number of points, *Tender Buttons* ironically invokes the
social rituals that mediate this human immersion in the world of
matter. "A Time to Eat" is described as "A pleasant simple habitual
and tyrannical and authorised and educated and resumed and articulate separation" (472). "A table means . . . a whole steadiness.
. . . A table means necessary places" (474). In stark contrast to the
"articulate separation" of the ritual of dining, "Food," the second
section of the text, celebrates the mixtures of diverse elements that
we actually consume: "A separation is not tightly in worsted and
sauce, it is so kept well and sectionally. Put it in the stew" (486).
Individual ingredients combine in stews and sauces. "It is not astonishing that bones mingle" (483). But in "Food," as in the
rest of *Tender Buttons*, concrete nouns and adjectives mingle in
more astonishing ways. "A cake, a real salve made of mutton and
liquor, a specially retained rinsing and an established cork and
blazing" transforms an ordinary dinner into an astonishingly un-
palatable menu (483). Although the individual foods named are
rather bland, the bill of fare includes such exotic items as a "but-
tered flower" and a "carpet steak"—delightful combinations that
can exist only in the realm of language (484, 488).

*Tender Buttons* begins by describing individual objects in
terms of others that are related by similarity or contiguity. As the
text progresses, however, its discourse becomes a combinative play
of purely linguistic possibilities. "What is" is challenged by what
one can "suppose," and some of these suppositions are mind-
stretching exercises in absurdity:

Supposing a certain time selected is assured, suppose it is even necessary, suppose no other extract is permitted and no more handling is needed, suppose the rest of the message is mixed with a very long slender needle and even if it could be any black border, supposing all this altogether made a dress and *suppose it was actual*, suppose the mean way to state it was occasional, if you suppose this in August and even more melodiously, if you suppose this even in the necessary incident of there certainly being no middle in summer and winter, suppose this and an elegant settlement a very elegant settlement is more than of consequence, it is not final and sufficient and substituted. This which was so kindly a present was constant. (466–67; my emphasis)

Every clause in this series is a correctly formed utterance; in this sense, they are all equally possible according to the grammatical rules of sentence formation. And the power of concrete nouns and adjectives forces the reader momentarily to "suppose it was actual," to imagine a message as a material entity, mixed with a needle and made into a dress. At times, in the midst of these absurd and impossible variations, the discourse suddenly reminds the reader that the words that it has been treating as playthings name objects that have a physical presence outside the realm of language:

Supposing there is a bone, there is a bone. Supposing there are bones. There are bones. When there are bones there is no supposing there are bones. There are bones and there is that consuming. (480)

The power of this discourse to threaten our habitual sense of the order of things depends on our recognition that the nouns it plays with name the objects that we see, touch, and eat.

Custom, "necessary places," would exclude this rich play of possibilities. The word "custom" recurs throughout *Tender Buttons* to invoke the habitual modes of order that it systematically defies. "Custom is in the centre," but the method of the text is to "[a]ct so that there is no use in a centre" (483, 498). The cubist painters' most subversive structural innovation was their absolute rejection of the time-honored convention of single-point perspective. Their paintings lack a privileged center; they provide no vantage point that allows the spectator's eye to resolve their iconography into familiar images of normalized human perception. The discourse of *Tender Buttons* "act[s] so that there is no use in a centre" in an analogous way. As it creates its mind-stretching combinations of nouns and adjectives, it deliberately refrains from constituting a human subject that would invite the reader to normalize them in terms of a psychological or narrative context. It asks questions, gives commands, and articulates a set of theoretical premises. But the discourse systematically refuses to present an authorial I/eye to serve as its origin and to guarantee its truth. "The author of all that is in there behind the door," teasing the reader with deliberate absence (499).

By compelling the reader to confront this idea that it is a structure that lacks a center, *Tender Buttons* most aggressively asserts it modernity.[14] Unseating both the subject and Western logic as privileged centers and guarantors of truth, this text deliberately flaunts the unlimited freeplay of substitution that is possible within the structure of language. Stein clearly conceived of language as a system of internal differences: "I and y and a d and a letter makes a change" (LGB, 106). She was acutely aware of the laws that govern sentence formation and of the ways in which they limit the possibilities of signification. *Tender Buttons* systematically demonstrates the idea that Nietzsche insistently expounded: "There is a philosophical mythology concealed in language."[15] In "'Reason' in Philosophy," he declared, "I fear we are not getting rid of God because we still believe in grammar."[16] In *Tender Buttons*, the play of substitution and combination takes place within the grammatical rules of sentence formation; this is what makes the text so subversive. By exploiting these inherently rational structures to "cause connections" that defy the most fundamental principles of logic, this text reduces to absurdity the fundamental philosophical assumptions that shape our use of language.

By the time she wrote *Tender Buttons*, Stein was far more convinced than William James, her first mentor, of the radical incompatibility between the order of language and the "truth" of unmediated sensory experience. In "Funes el memorioso" Borges created a character whose perfect perception and memory of detail made him virtually incapable of thought: "To think is to forget differences, to generalize, to abstract. In the over-stocked world of Funes there were only details, contiguous details."[17] The intense particularity of Funes's perceptions made him reject as too general even Locke's impossible dream of a language in which each individual object had its own name. In *Tender Buttons*, to write is to "practice the sign that means that really means a necessary betrayal" (468). In *Two* Stein had rejected all forms of rational ordering as reductions of the plenitude of immediate experience. She wrote *Tender Buttons* with a full awareness that even the act of naming entails a "necessary betrayal" of this "reality."

If even concrete nouns are a "betrayal," syntax is far more problematic, because of its inherently rational structure. If Stein had intended only to inventory the diverse contents of the "stream of consciousness," she could have written simple lists or polysyndetic series of nouns and adjectives. She occasionally used this form in *Tender Buttons*. But in general the text does not model the "stream" that James described as the structure of consciousness. In *Ulysses* Molly Bloom's soliloquy flows, but *Tender Buttons* is broken into a series of discrete and discontinuous pieces, separated by titles. In a recent essay, Italo Calvino proclaims the contemporary model of consciousness as "quite simply the revenge and triumph of all that is discontinuous, divisible and combinatory over continuous flux with its entire range of inter-related nuances."[18] He uses game theory and mathematical models to define the particular contemporaneity of this structural conception, but it is clearly prefigured both in cubist collage and in *Tender Buttons*. In Stein's text, this structure is dictated by her analysis of the order of language, not by a Jamesian conception of the "stream of consciousness." Its sentences are systematically patterned to foreground the most fundamental logical operations of syntax. But the freeplay of substitution and combination that these grammatical structures contain defies their inherent logical order.

"To be" is the verb most frequently used to forge connections among nouns in *Tender Buttons*.[19] In its copulative functions, this verb forms propositions of identity and predicates attributes or properties. The discourse of *Tender Buttons* depends on these copulative functions of the verb to "cause connections," but the propositions of identity it asserts refuse to make sense in any conventional way: "The sudden spoon is the wound in the decision" (471); "A shawl is a hat and hurt and a red balloon and an under coat and a sizer a sizer of talks" (475). *Tender Buttons* contains a multitude of these propositions of identity that are logically absurd. This copulative function of the verb "to be" is fundamental to definitions. Beginning with its opening section, *Tender Buttons* demonstrates the problem of defining the uniqueness of any object in language. Frequent repetition of the phrase "what is" systematically foregrounds this problem, while the discourse continues to demonstrate its denial of the logical principle of identity in every copulative sentence it creates.

The word "use" also recurs again and again, often in the phrase "what is the use." This repetition frequently emphasizes that the names of objects in this text are liberated from their normal subordination to human use and freed to enter the combinative play of the discourse: "There is no use there is no use at all in smell, in taste, in teeth, in toast, in anything, there is no use at all and the respect is mutual" (479). "Rooms" contains a brilliant demonstration of the inherent difficulty of defining objects in terms of their use (502). It begins with a plausible definition of a cape: "A cape is a cover." But a complication immediately emerges: "a cape is not a cover in summer." If a cape is to be defined by its function, then what is it when the weather precludes its use? The issue is resolved facetiously: "a cape is a cover and the regulation is that there is no such weather." Summer must be banished from this closed system of definition. But another problem arises, and again the issue is use: "A cape is not always a cover, a cape is not a cover when there is another." Finally, the discourse ironically concedes that "there is some use in not mentioning changing," but the point of the demonstration is clear. Definitions based on use are inadequate. No definition can account for the actual circumstances of any particular object. Like the sign, the definition is a "necessary betrayal" of the rich diversity of the external world.

The principle of causality is also under siege in *Tender Buttons*. "To make" is second only to the verb "to be" in the frequency of its occurrence in the text.[20] In logical discourse, this verb asserts relationships of cause and effect. In *Tender Buttons*, "A curving example makes righteous finger-nails" (508). Human actions and emotions have startling physical effects: "sincerely graciously trembling, sincere in gracious eloping, all this makes a furnace and a blanket" (480). Frequent repetition of the words "why" and "because" also serves to foreground the principle of causality, while the sentences in which they appear reduce it to absurdity: "Why should ancient lambs be goats and young colts and never beef, why should they, they should because there is so much difference in age" (480). The question "Why?" often stands alone, unanswered and unanswerable. Some of these questions are provocative: "Why is there so much resignation in a package" (502). Some are absurd: "why is there no oyster closer" (503). At one point this questioning turns back on itself: "Let us why, let us why weight, let us why winter chess, let us why why" (493). In "Rooms," the final section of *Tender Buttons*, the questions address the mysteries of man and nature: "why is there rain"; "Why is there so much useless suffering. Why is there" (502, 508). This persistent repetition of "why," in so many different contexts, acknowledges the perpetual human desire to assign causal explanations at the same time that it suggests the absence of any final cause that would arrest this incessant process of questioning.

The two other verbs that recur with a high degree of frequency in *Tender Buttons* are "to show" and "to mean." Like "to be" and "to make," they generally occur in lexical contexts that violate the logical processes of demonstration and interpretation:

> A white cup means a wedding. A wet cup means a vacation. A strong cup means an especial regulation. A single cup means a capital arrangement between the drawer and the place that is open. (484)

> The season gliding and the torn hangings receiving mending all
> this shows an example, it shows the force of sacrifice and like-
> ness and disaster and a reason. (501)

The semantic content of these and many other similar sentences
eludes the rational interpretive processes that the syntactical structures invoke. All the sentences in *Tender Buttons* serve as "examples" of the inherent logical order of language and the semantic
incongruity it can be forced to contain. But the discourse also insists
that "[a] sign is the specimen spoken" (483). The objects it names
are "specimens"; they are not symbols. They resist interpretation,
except as a parodic gesture: "The stamp that is not only torn but
also fitting is not any symbol. It suggests nothing" (501).

Norman Weinstein has suggested that "[T]he sentence has lost
its function in *Tender Buttons,* so its purpose is no longer purely
informational. The sentence is used as an aesthetic construct rather
than a logical, syntactical necessity."[21] The sentences in *Tender
Buttons* are certainly not "purely informational." But Weinstein's
comments fail to recognize how systematically this text patterns its
language to undermine the "logical, syntactical necessity" of the
sentence. Like Stein, the surrealists also used the sentence to bring
logically unrelated nouns together into fortuitous unions. But as
Lyotard has argued, their violations of sense do not seriously attack
language as a system.[22] The tension that Stein's text creates between its deliberate semantic disorder and its relentless repetition
of the fundamental grammatical structures of logical discourse systematically calls into question the order inherent in language. The
motifs of containment and closure recur throughout *Tender Buttons,* and the sentence is presented as the ultimate closed structure:
"A sentence of a vagueness that is violence is authority and a mis-
sion and stumbling and also certainly also a prison" (481). For
Stein, as for Nietzsche, the inherent logic of the sentence is the
"prison-house of language." Its authority delimits our thought.
The method of this text is to expose the laws that govern this
"prison" and to exploit their inherent force to consummate the
most arbitrary and violent unions within its confines. Each of its
sentences "is a spectacle, it is a binding accident" (468). No mat-

ter how "accidentally" its concrete nouns and adjectives are assembled, they are "bound" together by the conventional power of
syntax.

At the end of each of the first two sections of *Tender Buttons*,
the discourse uses another technique to subvert the imprisoning
system of language. Meanings come undone as words are separated
into clusters of phonemes: "bay labored," "be section," "sam in,"
"be where" (495, 493). "Easy" is transformed into "e c" (494).
"Alice" becomes "eel us" and "ale less" (494, 474). The word
"eating" generates the series "Eating he heat eating he heat it
eating, he heat it heat eating. He heat eating" (494). In *A Long Gay
Book* Stein wrote, "The doctrine which changed language was this,
. . . it was the language segregating" (LGB, 109). This disintegration of words powerfully demonstrates the fact that language is
a combinative system in which meaning is determined by internal
differences. At the end of "Objects," this assault on the stability
and coherence of words evokes suggestions of physical violence
and sexual aggression:

> Aider, why aider why whow, whow stop touch, aider whow,
> aider stop the muncher, muncher munchers.
> A jack in kill her, a jack in, makes a meadowed king,
> makes a to let. (TB, 476)

Near the end of "Food," the process of linguistic fragmentation
culminates in a powerful aesthetic statement which, itself, immediately disintegrates into non-sense:

> real is, real is only, only excreate, only excreate a no since.
> A no, a no since, a no since when, a no since when since,
> a no since when since a no since when since, a no since, a no
> since when since, a no since, a no, a no since a no since, a no
> since, a no since. (TB, 496)

Stein's pursuit of "reality" forced her to confront the irreconcilable difference between the order of language and the chaotic plenitude of immediate experience. As I emphasized earlier in this chapter, *Tender Buttons* claims that each of its "collections" of words
"shows the disorder, . . . it shows more likeness than anything

else." By the time she wrote this text, Stein's acute awareness of language as a "necessary betrayal," coupled with her continuing dedication to the "realism of the composition," had led her to conclude that, within language, "real is only, only excreate, only excreate a no since." Uniting the words creation and excretion, the verb "excreate" boldly asserts the inseparable connection between mind and matter. External to more conventional creativity, nonsense is the only viable model of the "real" that language can create.

*Tender Buttons* does not end with the kind of violent assaults on language that conclude the first two sections of the text. In "Rooms" the structures of words and sentences remain intact. The thematic interplay of separation and union continues to dominate the final portion of the text. But instead of culminating in disintegrative violence, "Rooms" builds to a final affirmation of harmonious union. Images of openness and spreading replace the boxes and other closed containers that dominate in "Objects," and the semantic field widens to encompass the world of nature as well as the man-made domestic interior. The natural world provides material for less problematic definitions—"Star-light, what is star-light, star-light is a little light that is not always mentioned with the sun, it is mentioned with the moon and the sun, it is mixed up with the rest of the time" (504)—perhaps because the question of "use" is irrelevant to something as distant as a star. Nature also suggests new metaphorical models for the creative process: "Nothing aiming is a flower. . . . Why is there more craving than there is in a mountain" (508). Restating its methods, the discourse reaffirms its power to create a purely poetic order: "centre no distractor, all order is in a measure" (506). Dance is used as another metaphor for the creative process: "Dance a clean dream and an extravagant turn up" (508). Language playfully combines the ballerina's turn-out with the homely turnip. No object is too lowly to join in this measured dance of words. *Tender Buttons* begins with a closed container; it ends with expansive natural images:[23]

The care with which the rain is wrong and the green is wrong and the white is wrong, the care with which there is a chair and plenty of breathing. The care with which there is incredible justice and likeness, all this make a magnificent asparagus, and also a fountain. (509)

By concluding with these images, *Tender Buttons* suggests an affinity between its artistic reordering of the familiar world and the fecund, replete harmony of nature that transcends the conceptual orders imposed by man. The poetic order it creates never claims to represent objective truth: "Claiming nothing, not claiming anything, not a claim in everything, collecting claimng, all this makes a harmony, it even makes a succession" (480). It asserts no facts; it does not solicit the reader's belief in the particular "harmonies" it creates. *Tender Buttons* is a playful text, a text to play with. What it offers is not truth but a joyous transgression of rationality, an imaginative liberation from our habitual sense of "reality": "all the pliable succession of surrendering makes an ingenious joy" (484). But the reader who surrenders to the lure of this playful and subversive discourse is challenged to reevaluate his customary idea of the order of "reality" and forced to recognize the extent to which it is shaped by the order of language.

In *Tender Buttons*, Stein joyfully embraced what she later identified as the "reality of the twentieth century . . . a time when everything cracks, where everything is destroyed, everything isolates itself" (P, 49). Later in her career she asserted that the "creator of the new composition in the arts is an outlaw until he is a classic," until the time when the "modern composition having become past is classified and the description of it is classical" (SW, 514). From our vantage point, we can readily situate *Tender Buttons* within the historical poetics of modernism. In Yeats's "Second Coming," "[t]hings fall apart; the center cannot hold." In *The Waste Land*, a "heap of broken images" is presented as the sum of human knowledge. Fragmentation and the loss of a center have become part of our "classical description" of the themes and structural principles of literary modernism. But Stein remained an "outlaw" long after writers like Yeats and Eliot were enshrined as "classics." The playful, domesticated disorder of *Tender Buttons* is strikingly different from the apocalyptic "rough beast" presaged by Yeats's vision of chaos or the spiritual aridity of Eliot's "waste land." In *Tender Buttons* the absence of a center is presented not as a loss but as a liberation that allows limitless invention of new, purely poetic orders.

Stein's earlier texts trace the arduous resistance that preceded this affirmation of the "reality of the twentieth century," which shaped all of her work after 1912. It is because her confrontation with this "reality" entailed such a radical critique of language that she still remains something of an "outlaw" in the Anglo-American literary tradition. In the texts that preceded *Tender Buttons*, she manipulated the material resources of language to embody her goal of "completed understanding." By the time she wrote *Tender Buttons*, she had left behind this pursuit of total knowledge in and through language and, with it, all nostalgic longing for this ideal. No longer conceived as an instrument for embodying external truth, language became her playground. Years later, she recalled the initial ecstasy of this liberation:

> I found myself plunged into a vortex of words, burning words, cleansing words, liberating words, feeling words, and the words were all ours, and it was enough that we held them in our hands to play with them; whatever you can play with is yours, and this was the beginning of knowing.[24]

This statement highlights the fundamental seriousness of Stein's most playful texts. They are all based on the premise that knowledge must begin with a knowledge of language. Rigorously investigating its laws and testing its limits, Stein's texts continue to challenge their readers to a new awareness of the system of language as both the necessary instrument and the inevitable "prison" of thought.

# Notes

## Introduction

1   Roman Jakobson's "On Realism in Art" brilliantly delineates the sets of mutually contradictory ideas that the term "realism" has been used to signify in the history of art. Jakobson's essay is translated in *Readings in Russian Poetics: Formalist and Structuralist Views*, ed. Ladislav Matejka and Krystyna Pomorska (Cambridge, Mass.: M.I.T. Press, 1971), pp. 39–47.

2   Richard Bridgman's *Gertrude Stein in Pieces* (New York: Oxford University Press, 1970) is the major exception. Bridgman's study, which undertakes the project of reading Stein's entire corpus, in its own terms, is exemplary in its insistence that a text like *Tender Buttons* will "yield its meanings as readers grow more familiar with it" (p. 125). Neil Schmitz's essay, "Gertrude Stein as Post-Modernist: The Rhetoric of *Tender Buttons*," *Journal of Modern Literature* 3, 5 (July 1974):1203–18, is another noteworthy exception. For a comprehensive survey of Stein criticism, see my bibliographical essay "Gertrude Stein," in *American Women Writers: Bibliographical Essays*, ed. Maurice Duke, Jackson R. Bryer, and M. Thomas Inge (Westport, Conn.: Greenwood Press, 1983), pp. 117–33.

3   Editorial, *Camera Work*, Special Number, August 1912.

4   John Malcolm Brinnin's elaboration of this analogy in *The Third Rose: Gertrude Stein and Her World* (Boston: Little, Brown and Co., 1959), p. 129, has been particularly influential. See also Michael J. Hoffman, *The Development of Abstractionism in the Writings of Gertrude Stein* (Philadelphia: University of Pennsylvania Press, 1965), p. 162.

5   Allegra Stewart, *Gertrude Stein and the Present* (Cambridge: Harvard University Press, 1967), p. 66.

6   Brinnin, *The Third Rose*, p. 134.

7   Wendy Steiner, *Exact Resemblance to Exact Resemblance: The Literary Portraiture of Gertrude Stein* (New Haven: Yale University Press, 1978), p. 160. Steiner's generic approach, which isolates the portraits from the chronological sequence of Stein's writings and derives Stein's theories of portraiture from her later writings, has evident historical weaknesses. In dealing with the crucial change from the early portraits to those in the style of *Tender Buttons*, her method can neither challenge nor surpass Stein's evasive treatment of this problem in her later essays.

Shortly after Steiner's study appeared, Marjorie Perloff further elaborated the correct analogy between Stein's writings of the *Tender Buttons* phase and "analytical" cubism in her essay "Poetry as Word-System: The Art of Gertrude

Stein," *American Poetry Review* 8 (September–October 1979); reprinted in her recent book *The Poetics of Indeterminacy: Rimbaud to Cage* (Princeton, N.J.: Princeton University Press, 1981), pp. 70–77.

8   David Antin, "Some Questions about Modernism," *Occident* 8, n.s. (spring 1974):31. In *Gertrude Stein: A Biography of Her Work* (New Haven: Yale University Press, 1951), Donald Sutherland also maintains that Stein was "influenced in some degree by the painting of Picasso, but rather as a corroboration than as a model" (p. 71).

9   These "Notebooks" are a collection of copybooks, schoolchildren's notebooks, and loose sheets of paper that contain Stein's working notes, written purely for her own use, between 1902 and 1911. They, along with a wealth of other Stein manuscripts, are part of the Yale Collection of American Literature. Leon Katz transcribed the "Notebooks" and established their chronology. A copy of his transcriptions is now available to scholars in the Beinecke Library.

In the following chapters I identify quotations from the "Notebooks" by citing the letter or number that Katz assigned to each one, followed by the page number of the individual notebook, as it is identified in Katz's transcripts. I reproduce the quotations exactly, with Stein's misspellings and idiosyncratic syntax intact. My only change is to capitalize proper names consistently.

As of 1973 Katz had established the following chronology for the notebooks I refer to in this study:

Summer 1908–December 1908 (*The Making of Americans* to page 149): Notebook 14, Notebook DB (the "Diagram Book"), Notebook MA.

January 1909–June 1909 (*The Making of Americans*, pages 150–285): Notebook 10, Notebooks A, B, C (continuous).

Summer 1909–December 1909 (*The Making of Americans*, pages 289–476): Notebooks D, E (continuous).

January 1910–Summer 1911 (*The Making of Americans*, pages 479–719): Notebook H; Notebook 13; Notebooks M, N (continuous).

10   The *Yale Catalogue*'s dating of the texts of this period, reproduced in appendix C of Bridgman's *Gertrude Stein in Pieces*, is often imprecise and frequently inaccurate. Leon Katz's painstaking research into Gertrude Stein's early career has done much to clarify the chronology of this period. Unless I indicate otherwise, I rely on the chronology Katz presents in "The First Making of *The Making of Americans*: A Study Based on Gertrude Stein's Notebooks and Early Versions of Her Novel (1902–1908)" (Ph.D. diss., Columbia University, 1963) and his dating of the notebooks. When my own study of the Stein archives at Yale and other sources has allowed me to clarify the dating of some of these texts more precisely, I present my evidence in footnotes.

11   Both Jean-François Lyotard, in *Discours, figure* (Paris: Klincksieck, 1971), and Iouri Lotman, in *La Structure du texts artistique*, ed. and trans. Henry Meschonnic (Paris: Gallimard, 1973), discuss the possibilities of iconicity or "figuration" in language. Readers of Lotman will recognize my general indebtedness to his conception of the work of art as a secondary model-building system, "with a double task of modeling the subject and the object simultaneously" (pp.

48–49). Lyotard's brilliant reexamination of the relationship between literature and painting, with its emphasis on the figural dimension of writing and the
conventional signs of painting, helped to clarify my approach to this problem.
Pierre Francastel's *La Figure et le lieu: L'Ordre visuel du Quattrocento* (Paris:
Gallimard, 1967) and his earlier studies also contributed to shaping my understanding of this issue in painting.

12  E. H. Gombrich, *Art and Illusion*, 2nd ed. (New York: Pantheon, 1969),
p. 313.

## Chapter 1   The "Reality" of Cézanne and Caliban

1  *The Tempest* 1.2.364–65.
2  Unsigned review in *Journal de Monaco* (October 30, 1906) and Gustave
Geffroy in *Le Journal* (October 17, 1905), both quoted in Ambroise Vollard,
*Paul Cézanne*, trans. Harold L. Van Doren (New York: Crown, 1937), pp.
124, 119. Chapter 12 of his book consists of excerpts from reviews of Cézanne
from 1895 to 1912 (pp. 115–26). Richard Shiff's recent essay "Seeing Cézanne," in *Critical Inquiry* 4, 4 (summer 1978):769–808, is a valuable study of
early critical responses to Cézanne's work in the context of theories of painting
current at the time.
3  Leo Stein, *Appreciations: Painting, Poetry, and Prose* (New York: Random
House, 1947), p. 58. James Mellow's *Charmed Circle: Gertrude Stein and
Company* (New York: Praeger, 1974) is the single most useful biography of
Stein. The most detailed information about the Steins' collection of painting
can be found in the essays, photographs, and exhibition catalogue in *Four
Americans in Paris: The Collections of Gertrude Stein and Her Family* (New
York: The Museum of Modern Art, 1970).
4  In *Matisse: His Art and His Public* (New York: The Museum of Modern Art,
1951), Alfred H. Barr, Jr., notes, "Ironically Max Weber remembers how in
1908 Matisse would speak of Cézanne to his pupils as 'le père de nous tous'"
(p. 87). I discuss what Barr calls the "crisis of 1907" in more detail in chapter 4,
in connection with Stein's portrait of Matisse.
5  Letter to Mabel Weeks, undated, in YCAL.
6  Quoted in Emile Bernard, "Paul Cézanne," *L'Occident* 6 (July 1904):23.
7  Quoted in Dore Ashton, *Picasso on Art: A Selection of Views* (New York:
Viking, 1972), p. 11.
8  This section of Stein's notebooks and some others that comment on Picasso and
other painters are reproduced in *Gertrude Stein on Picasso*, ed. Edward Burns
(New York: Liveright, 1970), pp. 96–97 and passim.
9  Gombrich, *Art and Illusion*, pp. 312–13; my emphasis.
10  Quoted in Linda Nochlin, *Realism and Tradition in Art, 1848–1900* (Engle-
wood Cliffs, N.J.: Prentice-Hall, 1966), pp. 48–49.
11  Quoted in Gombrich, *Art and Illusion*, pp. 297, 296.
12  Ibid., pp. 298, 321, and passim. Gombrich discusses Berkeley's *New Theory
of Vision* on p. 15 and elsewhere.

13  William James, *The Principles of Psychology* (1890; rpt. New York: Dover, 1950), 1:77, 2:243. James specifically invokes Ruskin's "innocence of the eye" in 2:179.

14  Maurice Denis, "Cézanne," in *Théories, 1890–1910: Du symbolisme et de Gauguin vers un nouvel ordre classique*, 4th ed. (Paris: L. Rouart et J. Watelin, 1920), p. 1.

15  Paul Cézanne, letter to Emile Bernard (July 25, 1904), in *Correspondance*, ed. John Rewald (Paris: Bernard Grasset, 1937), p. 265; my emphasis.

16  Ibid., p. 127.

17  Quoted in Bernard, "Paul Cézanne," p. 24.

18  Maurice Merleau-Ponty, "Cézanne's Doubt," in *Sense and Non-Sense*, trans. Hubert L. Dreyfus and Patricia Allen Dreyfus (Chicago: Northwestern University Press, 1964), p. 14. Max Kozloff, in *Cubism/Futurism*, suggests that Cézanne "wanted to graph the very fluctuations of seeing" (New York: Charterhouse, 1973), p. 24.

19  Quoted in Bernard, "Paul Cézanne," p. 23.

20  Quoted in Denis, "Cézanne," p. 253.

21  Ibid., pp. 258–59.

22  Lawrence Gowing, "The Logic of Organized Sensations," in *Cézanne: The Late Work*, ed. William Rubin (New York: The Museum of Modern Art, 1977), p. 66.

23  Clement Greenberg, "Cézanne and the Unity of Modern Art," *Partisan Review*, May–June 1951, pp. 327, 326, 328.

24  Quoted in Gerald L. Bruns, *Modern Poetry and the Idea of Language: A Critical and Historical Study* (New Haven: Yale University Press, 1974), p. 148.

25  Victor Shklovsky, "Art as Technique," in *Russian Formalist Criticism: Four Essays*, trans. Lee T. Lemon and Marion J. Reis (Lincoln: University of Nebraska Press, 1965), p. 12. In response to the nearly universal dissatisfaction with the Lemon and Reis translation of this passage, I have substituted the translation of this crucial final sentence that Frederic Jameson presents in *The Prison-House of Language* (Princeton, N.J.: Princeton University Press, 1972), p. 79. The Lemon and Reis translation of this sentence reads: "Art is a way of experiencing the artfulness of an object; the object is not important."

26  Stendhal, *Romans et nouvelles*, vol. 1, ed. Henri Martineau (Paris: Gallimard, 1952), p. 557.

27  Emile Zola, 1864 letter, quoted (in French) in Damon Grant, *Realism* (London: Methuen, 1970), p. 28.

28  Quoted in Grant, *Realism*, p. 42.

29  "La Société française allait être l'historien, je ne devais être que le secrétaire." Balzac, "Avant-propos," in *La Comédie humaine*, ed. Marcel Bouteron (Paris: Gallimard, 1951), 1:7. Elsewhere in the "Avant-propos" Balzac uses the metaphor of painting to describe his project (pp. 7, 8).

30  Roland Barthes, *Essais critiques* (Paris: Editions du seuil, 1964), p. 199.

31  Marcel Proust, "A propos du 'style' de Flaubert," *La Nouvelle Revue française* 7, 76, n.s. (January 1, 1920), p. 72.

## Chapter 2    *Three Lives*: The Realism of the Composition

1   In *Gertrude Stein in Pieces*, Richard Bridgman notes that Stein retained the title
    *Three Histories* until 1909, when her publisher persuaded her to change it to
    avoid confusion with his line of "real historical publications" (p. 46).

2   *Oeuvres complètes de Gustave Flaubert* (Paris: Club de l'Honnête Homme,
    1972), 4:22.

3   Richard Bridgman, *The Colloquial Style in America* (New York: Oxford Uni-
    versity Press, 1966), p. 46.

4   Dorrit Cohn, *Transparent Minds: Narrative Modes for Presenting Conscious-
    ness in Fiction* (Princeton, N.J.: Princeton University Press, 1978), p. 33.
    Hugh Kenner, *Joyce's Voices* (Berkeley: University of California Press, 1978),
    pp. 15–38.

5   Proust, "A propos du 'style' de Flaubert," pp. 73–74, 81. Cf. Alfred Thi-
    baudet's splendid chapter "Le style de Flaubert," in *Gustave Flaubert* (Paris:
    Librairie Plon, 1922), especially pp. 277–82, 304–17.

6   Bridgman, *Colloquial Style in America*, pp. 169–74. *Q.E.D.*'s reference to
    "Kate Croy" (*sic*) clearly indicates that Stein had read at least *The Wings of the
    Dove* before 1903.

7   These terms are taken from Dorrit Cohn's *Transparent Minds*. This excellent
    study establishes a well-defined (and much-needed) critical vocabulary for
    analyzing fictional representations of consciousness.

8   In *Flaubert: The Uses of Uncertainty* (London: Paul Elek, 1974), Jonathan
    Culler observes that Félicité is one of Flaubert's characters who "have no lan-
    guage which they could claim captures their existence, and this is what protects
    them, for as soon as the critic speaks of them he begins muttering clichés about
    the purity of simple folk, the joys of unalienated consciousness. . . . When she
    does speak to others the very banality of her discourse, its blatant exposure to
    irony, works to save it from any effective irony" (pp. 208–9).

9   Quoted in Hugh Kenner, *Samuel Beckett*, rev. ed. (Berkeley: University of
    California Press, 1968), p. 33.

10  See Leon Katz's introduction to the volume *Fernhurst, Q.E.D. and Other Early
    Writings*, pp. ix–xxxii.

11  Katz, "The First Making of *The Making of Americans*," p. 57.

12  The previous discussion of silence in *Q.E.D.* is indebted to an unpublished
    paper written by one of my students, Susan Abbott's "An Absence So Strange,
    a Presence So Vital: Issues of Lesbian Representation in Woolf, Stein, and
    Wittig." This paper, combined with a suggestion from Leon Katz, forced me to
    rethink my previous approach to the issue of irony in this text.

13  Bridgman notes the ironic effect of the repetition of the word "certainly"
    (*Colloquial Style in America*, pp. 181–82).

14  Note to "The Thorn" (1800), in *Poetical Works of William Wordsworth*, ed.
    Ernest de Selincourt and Helen Darbishire (Oxford: Clarendon Press, 1940–
    49), 2:513. Frances Ferguson's discussion of Wordsworth's writings about
    language in chapter 1 of *Wordsworth: Language as Counter-Spirit* (New Ha-
    ven: Yale University Press, 1977) brought this passage to my attention (pp.
    11–16).

## Chapter 3    History as Repetition: *The Making of Americans*

1    "The Making of Americans," published in *Fernhurst, Q.E.D. and Other Early Writings*. Leon Katz's introduction briefly discusses the genesis of Stein's project. Katz's "First Making of *The Making of Americans*" is a thorough study of the early stages of the novel.

2    Sören Kierkegaard, *Repetition*, trans. Walter Lowrie (Princeton, N.J.: Princeton University Press, 1946), pp. 33–34.

3    Balzac, "Avant-propos," pp. 3–5.

4    Otto Weininger, *Sex and Character* (London: William Heinemann; New York: G. P. Putnam's Sons, 1906), p. 83. Leon Katz's recent essay, "Weininger and *The Making of Americans*," *Twentieth Century Literature* 24, 1 (spring 1978): 8–26, presents a useful account of the importance of Weininger's book for Stein.

5    P. 297.

6    E.g., MOA, 172, 199.

7    Emile Benveniste, "Les Relations de temps dans le verbe français," in *Problèmes de linguistique générale* (Paris: Gallimard, 1966), pp. 237–50. "De la subjectivité dans le langage" and "La Nature des prenoms," in the same volume, provide a more detailed study of the nature of the "I" constituted by the discourse. Gérard Genette's "Frontières du récit," in *Figures II* (Paris: Editions du Seuil, 1969), uses Benveniste's study of tense and pronouns in his suggestive discussion of the limits of narration.

8    John Lyons observes this fact of usage in his discussion of aspect in his *Introduction to Theoretical Linguistics* (Cambridge: Cambridge University Press, 1969), pp. 315–16. Stein also regularly uses the verbs "feel" and "love," which Lyons classifies as stative, in the progressive aspect. I have also relied on Bernard Comrie's *Aspect: An Introduction to the Study of Verbal Aspect and Related Problems* (Cambridge: Cambridge University Press, 1976) for my understanding of this characteristic feature of Stein's syntax.

9    Roland Barthes, *Le Plaisir du texte* (Paris: Editions du Seuil, 1973), pp. 25–26.

10    Patricia Tobin, *Time and the Novel: The Genealogical Imperative* (Princeton, N.J.: Princeton University Press, 1978), pp. 7, 85.

11    Quoted in *Faulkner in the University*, ed. F. L. Gwynn and J. L. Blotner (Charlottesville: University of Virginia Press, 1959), p. 107.

12    Linda Jeanne McMiniman, "Design and Experiment in *The Making of Americans* by Gertrude Stein" (Diss., University of Pennsylvania, 1976), p. 124. In chapter 4, McMiniman makes effective use of transformational grammar in her analysis of the characteristic syntax of Stein's long sentences. Her discussion of the larger structures of Stein's prose, in the same chapter, is also valuable.

13    See pp. 3–4, above. This notebook analysis of various relationships to the object finds its way into the novel in the Alfred Hersland chapter (e.g., MOA, 579, 587). In NB-A, 10; D, 10–11, 15; E, 12, Stein explicitly identifies herself with the "earthy" realism of Cézanne and Picasso.

14    Alfred H. Barr, Jr., *Picasso: Fifty Years of His Art* (New York: The Museum of Modern Art, 1946), p. 57.

15  John Golding, *Cubism: A History and an Analysis, 1907–1914* (New York: Harper and Row, 1959), pp. 47–60.

16  Quoted in Bernard, "Paul Cézanne," p. 24.

17  See William Rubin, "Cézannism and the Beginnings of Cubism," in *Cézanne: The Late Work*, ed. Rubin, pp. 201–2, n. 150. Rubin's essay is the major source for my discussion of the relationship between Picasso's work and Cézanne's.

18  Five letters Picasso wrote to Stein in the summer of 1909 mention that he is sending Stein photographs of his paintings (nos. 22, 23, 28, 29, 32 in the Picasso/Stein correspondence file in YCAL, dated May [?] 1909 [?]; May 1909; 24 June 1909; 28 August 1909; end of August 1909). A later letter (no. 36, spring [?] 1909) promises to send a photo of the portrait of Vollard as soon as it is completed.

19  Leo Stein, *Appreciations*, pp. 140–41.

20  One of her notebooks is labeled "Diagram Book." Occasionally, she drew diagrams of the various "layers" of individuals she was analyzing. Cf. MOA, 225, 595.

21  John Berger, *The Moment of Cubism and Other Essays* (New York: Pantheon Books, 1969), p. 20.

22  *Collected Papers of Charles Sanders Peirce*, ed. Charles Hartshorne and Paul Weiss (Cambridge: Harvard University Press, 1933), 4:359.

23  The anecdote appears in MOA, 489–90.

24  Kierkegaard, *Repetition*, p. 34.

25  Gilles Deleuze, *Différence et répétition* (Paris: Presses Universitaires de France, 1968), pp. 7, 8.

26  I am indebted to Michel Foucault's "Classifying," chapter 5 of *The Order of Things* (1966; English trans., New York: Random House, 1970), particularly his discussion of "Character" (pp. 138–45).

27  In ABT Stein recalls that she finished the novel and then began *A Long Gay Book* and *Many Many Women* "at the same time" (113). In fact, MOA clearly indicates that she began serious work on *A Long Gay Book* while she was working on the Alfred Hersland chapter: "I am going to write a book and it will be a very long one and it will be all full up, completely filled up with pairs of them twos of them, . . . twos of men, of women, of women and men, of men and women" (549). This indicates precisely the point at which she began serious work on *A Long Gay Book*. Stylistic considerations suggest that the first few paragraphs of this text may have been written several years earlier.

28  Freud's idea that the compulsion to repeat was "more primitive, more elementary, more instinctual than the pleasure principle which it overrides" led him to associate it with the death instinct. For Freud, any "instinct is an urge inherent in organic life to restore an earlier state of things which the living entity has been obliged to abandon under the pressure of external disturbing forces." (*Beyond the Pleasure Principle*, trans. and ed. James Strachey [New York: Liveright, 1961], pp. 17, 30).

29  According to Leon Katz, "During the writing of the Alfred Hersland chapter at the end of 1910, Gertrude all but abandoned the book while she worked out her descriptive problems in a series of portraits" ("The First Making of *The Making*

*of Americans,"* p. 247). Katz dates this chapter January 1910 to late summer 1911.

## Chapter 4    Portraits of Artists and Others

1   Bridgman, *Gertrude Stein in Pieces*, pp. 210–11.

2   Katz bases his dating of this portrait on a letter from Harriet Levy to Gertrude Stein (December 31, 1910) that mentions "Ada" ("The First Making of *The Making of Americans,"* pp. 144–45, 247. One of Stein's letters speaks of plans for a volume: "I have been writing quite a number of portrait sketches and in a little while I will have enough to make a small book and I would like so much to make some arrangement with you" (rough draft of a letter from Stein to George Doran, which Doran answered March 2, 1911; both are in YCAL).

3   See Christian Zervos, *Pablo Picasso: Oeuvres* (Paris, 1942–67), vol. 6, reproductions of sketches 1118–20 and paintings 162–76, for a pictorial record of this process of reduction to essential structural elements. These sketches and paintings represent the progressive reduction of three female heads, as follows: (a) 1118, 165, 170, 172; (b) 1120, 168, 171; (c) 1118, 167, 169, 174, 175, 176.
     Robert Rosenblum's *Cubism and Twentieth-Century Art*, 2nd ed. (New York: Harry N. Abrams, 1966), contains an excellent study of Picasso's portrait style between 1909 and 1911 (pp. 36–67).

4   Edward Fry, *Cubism* (New York: McGraw-Hill, 1966), p. 20.

5   Bridgman was the first critic to note that the repetition of the word "gay" "turns ragged and hysterical as Miss Furr tries to endure her rejection, making this a pathetic portrait rather than, as both Elizabeth Sprigge and Carl Van Vechten have found it, a 'charming' one" (*Gertrude Stein in Pieces*, p. 95).

6   A letter from Stein to *The English Review* announces that she is sending the portraits of Picasso and Matisse. The reply from the magazine, written by Austin Harrison, is dated August 25, 1911. Although the David Hersland chapter contains many echoes of these portraits (see especially MOA, 890, para. 3–5), clearly they were written before she began this section of *The Making of Americans*.

7   Hoffman, *The Development of Abstractionism*, p. 165.

8   No. 37 in the Stein Collection in YCAL. Words are crossed out, as shown, in the manuscript.

9   Quoted in Lincoln Kirstein, *Elie Nadelman* (New York: Eakins Press, 1973), p. 267. Kirstein quotes Stein's notebook entries as the "most vivid portrait of young Nadelman" (pp. 190–91).

10  Quoted in ibid., p. 265. first published in *Camera Work* 32 (October 1910).

11  Quoted in Kirstein, *Elie Nadelman*, p. 198. In 1908 Leo Stein took Picasso to see Nadelman's drawings. Nadelman later claimed that cubism was merely an imitation of his work (ibid., pp. 183–84).

12  Barr, *Matisse*, p. 124. Barr's book and his essay "Matisse, Picasso, and the Crisis of 1909," *Magazine of Art* 44 (May 1951):163–70, are the major sources for my discussion of Matisse in this chapter.

13  Michael and Sarah Stein were lifelong patrons and intimate friends of Matisse.

See Lucile M. Golson, "The Michael Steins of San Francisco: Art Patrons and Collectors," in *Four Americans in Paris*, pp. 35–49.

14  Quoted in Barr, *Matisse*, p. 119; my emphasis. This essay, which Barr describes as "Matisse's most complete and important statement about art," was first published in *La Grande Revue* (Paris), December 25, 1908. Barr's book contains the English translation (pp. 119–23).

15  NB-A, 13–14. Sarah Stein's lecture notes are reproduced in Barr, *Matisse*, p. 552.

16  Quoted in Barr, *Matisse*, p. 121; my emphasis.

17  Ibid., p. 122.

18  Quoted in Ashton, *Picasso on Art*, p. 164.

## Chapter 5   "The Complete Connection": *Two* and Other Transitional Texts

1  NB-MA, 23, quoted in Katz, "Weininger and *The Making of Americans*," p. 16.

2  In a letter written to me in October 1975, Leon Katz argued that Stein's notebook analyses of her brother Leo, which I discuss later in this chapter, contributed to the characterization of David Hersland and that Stein was working on *Two* at the same time she was writing this chapter of the novel. In my 1975 dissertation, I assumed that the analysis of Leo and *Two* were both written after the novel was completed. My subsequent study of these texts led me to accept Katz's dating, which illuminated my reading of these two works.

3  NB-MA, 23, quoted in Katz, "Weininger and *The Making of Americans*," p. 16.

4  The passage I quoted above (MOA, 779–80) is directly preceded by a sentence transcribed from this section of her notebooks (NB-M, 30): "To some spirituality and idealism have no meaning excepting as meaning completest intensification of any experiencing, any conception of transcending experience has to some not any meaning."

5  William James, "The Sentiment of Rationality," first published in 1898, reprinted in *Essays on Faith and Morals* (Cleveland: Meridian, 1962), p. 70.

6  Weininger, *Sex and Character*, pp. 192–93. In "Weininger and *The Making of Americans*," Leon Katz argues that Stein, "during the writing of *The Making of Americans*, was in full flight from James and from pragmatism" (p. 24). Without discounting the evidence he presents of Stein's intentional break with Jamesian pragmatism, I want to emphasize how much her methods always remained rooted in James's teachings, even during this period of conscious rebellion against some of his precepts.

7  James, "Reflex Action and Theism," first published in 1881, reprinted in *Essays*, p. 117. The quotations in the next sentence are also taken from this essay (pp. 118–19).

8  Quoted in Mabel Dodge Luhan, *Movers and Shakers* (New York: Harcourt, Brace, 1936), p. 32. Stein's correspondence with Mabel Dodge, reprinted in this volume, contains some invaluable information about the chronology of her work during this time. On November 2, 1911, she wrote, "The long book is

finished." In the letter containing the description of *Two*, Stein reported on the current state of her various projects: "I am working on four books now. One is a long gay book and has lots and lots of everything in it and goes on. It will be quite long. I have written about 120 pages of it. Another is a study of two, a man and a woman having the same means of expression and the same emotional and spiritual experiences with different qualities of intellect. That is going very well and slowly. Then I am doing one that will be published in a couple of months that consists of many portraits of women. Then I am doing another which is a description of a family of five who are all peculiar and are in a peculiar relation each one to every other one of the five of them. This one is just fairly begun." This letter is undated, but it refers to the futurist exhibition at Bernheims, which took place February 5–12, 1912 (Umbro Apollonio, ed., *Futurist Manifestos* [New York: Viking, 1973], p. 220). This progress report reveals that in February 1912 *Many Many Women* was nearing completion; *Two* and *A Long Gay Book* were in progress; and *Jenny, Helen, Hannah, Paul and Peter* was just begun. Apparently, Stein had not yet begun work on *G.M.P.* The style of *Many Many Women* suggests that it was, indeed, the first to be finished, as Stein planned.

*Two* was the second of these texts to be completed, before June of 1912. A letter from Georgiana King in YCAL, postmarked Madrid, June 18, 1912, informed Stein that she was returning the manuscript of *Two*.

9 Bridgman discusses it briefly, in *Gertrude Stein in Pieces* (pp. 112–14); Hoffman, in *The Development of Abstractionism*, equally briefly (pp. 156–61). In a conversation with Leon Katz at a very early stage of my work on Stein, he emphasized the importance of this text for understanding Stein's development during these years. More recently, in "Spreading the Difference: One Way to Read Gertrude Stein's *Tender Buttons*," *Twentieth Century Literature* 24, 1 (spring 1978):57–75, Pamela Hadas uses this text to support her clever but inevitably reductive reading of *Tender Buttons* as a "personal story" of Gertrude Stein's break with Leo and her love for Alice.

10 Cf. NB-I, 14; C, 23.

11 Manuscript #35 in YCAL.

12 Katz, "Weininger and *The Making of Americans*," pp. 8–9.

13 "Leo says Matisse's esthetic quality is clarity" (NB-13, 11). "When Leo said all classification is teleological I knew I was not a pragmatist" (NB-D, 11).

14 Leo Stein, *Journey into the Self* (New York: Crown Publishers, 1950), p. 48.

15 Mellow (*Charmed Circle*) discusses the dating of this event on p. 205. Based on his interviews with Alice B. Toklas, Leon Katz has been able to determine that, although Leo did not move out of the rue de Fleurus until 1913, the actual separation took place as early as the late spring or early summer of 1911, when Leo moved to Florence Blood's villa in Fiesole. This information, which I received only recently, confirmed my sense that *Two* was very much a part of Stein's process of separating from her brother.

16 Catharine R. Stimpson's essay "The Mind, the Body, and Gertrude Stein," *Critical Inquiry* 3, 3 (spring 1977):489–506, is the first serious effort to deal with the question of Stein's sexual identity as it manifests itself in her writing, in the context of her historical situation. Stimpson discusses the masculinization apparent in Stein's earliest texts and in *The Autobiography of Alice B. Toklas*,

but she does not discuss this countermovement of feminization.

17   Manuscript notes indicate that Stein wrote this piece as a direct contrast to the portrait of Nadelman: "like Nadelman relation of ideas to impulse to temperament to morality" (#7 in YCAL). Like the man in *Two*, Nadelman is portrayed as a man who fails as an artist because of an excess of "thinking."

18   Earlier in *Two*, manuscript notes clarify that Stein was contrasting her brother Leo's religious experiences with "Jane's." We know that Sally Stein was an ardent Christian Scientist. It is possible, as Leon Katz has suggested in correspondence with me, that Stein's initial intention here was to mimic Sally's religious rhetoric. But, whatever the author's intentional "meaning" (and, as I have been demonstrating in this chapter, Stein was deliberately loosening her conscious control of her writing in this text), the "significance" of this passage within the text, for the reader, is a celebration of those qualities of the woman's experience that the male character so strikingly lacks.

19   B. F. Skinner, "Has Gertrude Stein a Secret?" *Atlantic Monthly* 153 (January 1934):50–57.

20   André Breton, *Manifestes du surréalisme* (Paris: Gallimard, 1966), p. 37.

21   EA, 30; P, 43.

22   "In Spain Gertrude Stein began to write the things that led to Tender Buttons" (ABT, 115). This was the summer of 1912. Describing this trip in ABT, she mentions meeting Georgiana King (see note 8, above) and seeing the dancer called the Argentina. A manuscript note for *G.M.P.* (at what is page 227 of the printed text) mentions Argentina. A number of details in the section I quote seem to describe a Spanish setting.

23   Manuscript #42 in YCAL.

24   ABT states that Stein wrote most if not all of *Tender Buttons* shortly after she returned to Paris after her summer in Spain: "after the return to Paris she described objects, she described rooms and objects, which joined with her first experiments done in Spain, made the volume *Tender Buttons*" (119). But later in the *Autobiography*, discussing three manuscripts submitted to Donald Evans for publication, Stein recalled that "two had been written during our first trip to Spain and Food, Rooms, etcetera, immediately on our return" (156). The two accounts are slightly contradictory. I am fairly certain that she wrote *Tender Buttons* only after her "*first* experiments done in Spain," in *G.M.P.* A letter to Mabel Dodge written in February 1913 describes her projects at that time as follows: "The long gay book goes on very well. Another one of the five is finished, so is the one of the Two. I am doing a short thing of Scenes. Then I am doing two very short ones about the English and about the Publishers, the British Museum and the Portrait Gallery, the long one about the whole Paris crowd goes on slowly" (35). The "long one about the whole Paris crowd" must be *G.M.P.*: both this text and *A Long Gay Book* have always been dated earlier than this. "Scenes" and "Publishers," two of the other texts described in this letter, are stylistically very similar to *Tender Buttons*; both were written during her trip to England early in 1913. Apparently *Tender Buttons* was completed before this letter was written. On the basis of this evidence I have dated it 1912 in my study, although it could have been completed a few weeks after the end of the year.

## Chapter 6 *Tender Buttons*: "The Music of the Present Tense"

1 Brinnin, *The Third Rose*, p. 142; Norman Weinstein, *Gertrude Stein and the Literature of the Modern Consciousness* (New York: Frederick Ungar, 1970), p. 66.

2 *Four Americans in Paris*, plates 19, 44, 45, 47. Cf. photos of the Steins' studio (ca. 1913) on pp. 92–93.

3 Meyer Schapiro, *Paul Cézanne*, 3rd ed. (New York: Harry N. Abrams, 1965), pp. 14–15.

4 According to Douglas Cooper, in *The Cubist Epoch* (London: Phaidon Press, 1970), p. 54, this innovation first appeared in Braque's *The Portuguese*.

5 This event was traditionally dated as 1911–12, but more recently, after conversations with Picasso, Douglas Cooper established this more precise dating (ibid., p. 58).

6 In Roman Jakobson and Morris Halle, *The Fundamentals of Language* (The Hague: Mouton, 1956), pp. 55–82. David Lodge's recent book, *The Modes of Modern Writing: Metaphor, Metonymy, and the Typology of Modern Literature* (Ithaca, N.Y.: Cornell University Press, 1977), also uses Jakobson's bipolar model to describe the extremes of Stein's styles in *The Making of Americans* and *Tender Buttons*. Randa K. Dubnick's "Two Types of Obscurity in the Writings of Gertrude Stein," *Emporia State Research Studies* 24, 3 (winter 1976):5–27, employs the same model. Neither one goes beyond this initial application of the two extremes of aphasic speech to explore the interplay of metaphor and metonymy at other levels of structure in Stein's texts.

7 Jakobson, "Two Aspects of Language," pp. 78–79.

8 Rosenblum, *Cubism and Twentieth-Century Art*, p. 60.

9 Jakobson, "Two Aspects of Language," pp. 85–86.

10 Ibid., p. 92.

11 Dubnick argues that the "metaphorical type of association seems to predominate in *Tender Buttons*, as one might expect," given Jakobson's model ("Two Types of Obscurity," p. 29). But this is clearly not the case. Stein's early style also reverses the normal semantic expectations that Jakobson associates with the other pole of discourse. Jakobson characterizes realist fiction as metonymic, because the narrator moves from one topic to another "following the path of contiguous associations. . . . [H]e metonymically digresses from the plot to the atmosphere and from the characters to the setting in space and time. He is fond of synecdochic details" (Jakobson, "Two Aspects of Language," p. 92). While it systematically refuses to name things directly, Stein's early prose constantly creates equivalences through phonemic, lexical, and syntactical repetition. Instead of proceeding in a linear, "contiguous" manner from one topic to another, it revolves endlessly around the same axis, spinning out minute variations on the same theme.

12 Richard Bridgman's reading of *Tender Buttons* in *Gertrude Stein in Pieces* emphasizes the recurrence of word clusters in the text: "colors predominate, especially versions of red—pink, scarlet, crimson, rose. There are also words of transparency: glass, spectacle, eye glasses, carafe. Images of opening are common: gate, window. There are also ones of closing and obscurity: glaze, dusty,

curtain, cover. One cluster of words concerns polishing and its effect: rubbing, shining, glittering. There are numerous receptacles: cups, plates, sacks. And there are images of breakage: crack, separate, shatter. These images of unity and separation, of obscurity and dirt, of clear vision and cleanliness, of blockage and of opening, of containers and of holders are all involved in the thematic development of *Tender Buttons*. Whatever the errors in their interpretation, their presence is undeniable and must be the starting-point for understanding the book" (p. 126).

13  Alain Robbe-Grillet, *Pour un nouveau roman* (Paris: Gallimard, 1963), p. 81. The term "littérature objective" is from Roland Barthes's 1955 essay with the same title, reprinted in *Essais critiques*, pp. 29–40. Although Robbe-Grillet later began describing his work as a "subjectivité totale" (p. 148), his early essays clearly set forth an ideal of objectivity.

14  Jacques Derrida has identified this kind of "decentering," which rejects the notion of any certain presence that exists outside of structure, as characteristic of the modern era. He associates this "rupture" with the "moment . . . when language invaded the universal problematic, . . . when, in the absence of a center or an origin, everything became discourse. . . . that is to say everything became a system in which the central signified, the originary or transcendental signified, is never absolutely present outside a system of differences. The absence of the transcendental signified infinitely extends the field and the play of signification" ("La Structure, le signe, et le jeu dans le discours des sciences humaines," in *L'Ecriture et la différence* [Paris: Seuil, 1967], pp. 409–11).

15  From *The Wanderer and His Shadow* (1880), quoted in Friedrich Nietzsche, *Twilight of the Idols and the Anti-Christ*, trans. R. J. Hollingdale (London: Penguin Books, 1968), p. 191.

16  *Twilight of the Idols*, p. 38.

17  "Sospecho, sin embargo, que no era muy capaz de pensar. Pensar es olvidar diferencias, es generalizar, abstraer. En el abarrotado mundo de Funes no había sino detalles, casi inmediatos" (Jorge Luis Borges, *Ficciones* [Buenos Aires: Emecé Editores, 1956], p. 126).

18  Italo Calvino, "Notes toward a Definition of the Narrative Form as a Combinative Process," trans. Bruce Merry, *Twentieth Century Studies* 3 (May 1970):95.
    Neil Schmitz's essay "Gertrude Stein as Post-Modernist" is the only previous treatment of *Tender Buttons* to address the "core of its linguistic pact" (p. 1204). Correctly rejecting Brinnin's and Hoffman's analogies between Stein's work and cubist painting, Schmitz too readily dismisses the paintings themselves in his argument that *Tender Buttons* is a *post*-modernist work, unrelated to the aesthetics of cubism. As my comparative references in this chapter and elsewhere indicate, I see more continuity than rupture between the "modernism" of Stein and Picasso and both "post-modernist" literature and "poststructuralist" literary theory.

19  In *Gertrude Stein: A Biography of Her Work*, Donald Sutherland noted that Stein's "constant use of *is* or *makes* as the main verb is a simple sum or equation" (p. 95).

20  It seems important to emphasize the pervasiveness of the verbs I discuss in this

section. A rough count indicates that "to make" occurs 95 times in the text; "to show," 93 times; "to mean," 59 times. Forms of the verb "to be" appear 382 times. "To have" is the only other frequent verb (60). Miscellaneous verbs total only 377.

21 Weinstein, *Gertrude Stein and the Literature of the Modern Consciousness*, p. 64.

22 "No attack on language as a system, only violations within the utterance. And at least in the case of Breton, the violations are exclusively semantic [*Pas d'atteinte à langue, seulement des dérogations de parole. Et chez Breton au moins, exclusivement semantique*]" (Lyotard, *Discours, figure*, p. 325; cf. p. 289). For Breton, the "light of the image" is the essential power of surrealist writing, and the most forceful images are those that represent the highest degree of arbitrariness in the "two realities" they bring together (*Manifestes du surréalisme*, pp. 50–51).

23 Allegra Stewart first noted this, in *Gertrude Stein and the Present*, p. 132.

24 "American Language and Literature" (1944), manuscript #548 in YCAL.

# Index

Library of Congress Cataloging in Publication Data
Walker, Jayne L., 1944–
The making of a modernist.
Includes bibliographical references and index.
1. Stein, Gertrude, 1874–1946—Criticism and interpre-
tation. 2. Stein, Gertrude, 1874–1946—Knowledge—Art.
I. Title.
PS3537.T323Z88   1984     818'.5209     83–18184
ISBN 0–87023–323–8